ROUTLEDGEFALMER STUDIES IN HIGHER EDUCATION

PHILIP G. ALTBACH, *General Editor*

TEACHER EDUCATION FOR CRITICAL CONSUMPTION OF MASS MEDIA AND POPULAR CULTURE

Stephanie A. Flores-Koulish, Ph.D.

RoutledgeFalmer
New York & London

Published in 2005 by
RoutledgeFalmer
270 Madison Avenue
New York, NY 10016
www.routledge-ny.com

Published in Great Britain by
RoutledgeFalmer
2 Park Square
Milton Park, Abingdon
Oxon, OX14 4RN
www.routledge.co.uk

RoutledgeFalmer is an imprint of the Taylor & Francis Group.

Printed in the United States of America on acid-free paper.

Library of Congress Cataloging-In-Publication Data

Flores-Koulish, Stephanie A., 1966–
    Teacher education for critical consumption of mass media and popular culture / by
Stephanie A. Flores-Koulish.
        p. cm.—(RoutledgeFalmer studies in higher education)
    Originally presented as the author's thesis (Ph. D.—Boston College).
    Includes bibliographical references and index.
    ISBN 0-415-94999-8 (hardback : alk. paper)
    1. Media literacy—United States. 2. Mass media in education—United States.
3. Popular culture—Study and teaching (Elementary) 4. Critical pedagogy—United
States. 5. Elementary school teachers—Training of—United States—Case studies.
I. Title. II. Series: RoutledgeFalmer studies in higher education (Unnumbered)
    P96.M42U584 2005
    302.23'0973—dc22   2005012979

For Olivia

Contents

Acknowledgments

Upon reaching the end of this I could not help but ponder the social construction of dissertation writing. Must we really become as worked up and stressed out about this process as everyone says we should? I have no precise answer, but I must admit my own falling into the trap at times. But having fallen and risen, I now thankfully have the opportunity to pay tribute to some of the many wonderful people who helped me along the "marathon" miles.

Let me begin with Tom Keating, my chair, advisor and friend. I so appreciated your kindness, attentiveness, constant support, and challenges. You respectfully allowed me the independence I craved yet you continued to push me for clarification. Thank you.

To Tim Lensmire, I feel fortunate to have had your assistance as a reader, an advocate, and as someone I needed to push me in new directions. Thank you.

To Ana Martinez Aleman, another reader, your dedication and depth encouraged me to dig deeply, and your assistance in my research process helped propel me at opportune times. Gracias.

To my many fine professors at Boston College, Marilyn Cochran Smith, Ann Marie Barry, Lillie Albert, Jerry Pine, Otherine Neisler, Michael Schiro, Sara Freedman, I thank you for the knowledge and guidance you shared with me.

To the Boston College administration, I am appreciative for the generous fellowship support during my time there.

To my Boston College cohort of 1998, I am ever-grateful for all that you know and who you are, particularly Jennifer Gallo-Fox and Julie Zoino!

To Mimi Coughlin, I'm glad we held hands in the last few miles of the race; your insights and humor helped get me here.

To Hayley Haberman and Bill Mueller, I thank you for your support and friendship, and Hayley, for your students' important opinions.

To Rob and Andrew Flores, my favorite nephews, thank you for helping me learn about what kids like to watch on television.

To Smitty, I thank you for your help in video reproduction, but more importantly, I really appreciated your friendship and ears for listening to my ramblings during this process.

To "Beatrice," "Nadia," "Mary Beth," "Michelle," and "Beth," without your thoughtful participation, the dissertation on which this book is based would not exist.

To Jo Ann Moody and the New England Board of Higher Education, I thank you for your fellowship support during this last year.

To the many fine folks at the University of Vermont, I will have long-lasting special memories of a great year spent there, professionally and personally.

To Sr. Rose Pacatte, you're inspirational—thanks for the many free convent meals and great media literacy conversation.

To Rob Koulish, my best friend, my life long colleague and partner. I love you for everything that you are. Thank you for your support and belief in me.

And lastly, to Do, Happy 86th birthday—May 10th 2002.

Stephanie A. Flores-Koulish
Assistant Professor
Curriculum & Instruction
Loyola College in Maryland

Foreword

The biggest challenge to *media literacy education* is its title. To the un-initi-ated, it sounds boring and boring is anathema to the postmodern audience regardless of where we find it–in front of the television, in the classroom, or at your local online university.

Media literacy education is, however, the great educational hope of our times for two reasons. The first is because it brings into sharp focus the need for teachers and students to integrate curriculum content and contem-porary culture through critical engagement; the second is because media lit-eracy education as both content and process *per force* makes students and teachers co-learners. If educators are mindful of this, together they can de-velop skills to both navigate and create the entertainment and information media popular culture in which we all live, breathe, move and have our being. The next Steven Spielberg, Nielsen family, American president, Mother Teresa, Martha Stewart, Oprah and teachers are in our midst. I ask myself what this reality means for education today and today's educators. Flores-Koulish's book is a useful guide to arriving at an adequate and appro-priate response that respects the human person.

I first met Stephanie Flores-Koulish at the National Media Education Conference in Colorado Springs, CO in 1998. I had recently completed my MA in Education in Media Studies at the University of London's Institute of Education and Stephanie was just beginning her doctoral studies in Curriculum and Instruction with a concentration on media literacy educa-tion at Boston College. Since we were both living in the Boston area we spent many hours talking about media literacy education and how we could com-municate it to teachers and parents.

Stephanie's doctoral dissertation examines what a group of undergrad-uate elementary education students knows and understands about media in the world and how this group might, or might not, integrate that knowledge into their future teaching. Their attitudes about media and popular culture provoke inquiry and dialogue about the future institutionalization of media literacy education in schools of education. The research is innovative, accessible, practical and rich and is of interest to schools of education, communication, institutes of popular culture and media literacy educators.

The results of Stephanie's research are important for me because they question the critical self-awareness of preservice teachers in content areas and promote reflection for possible future praxis. In addition, her work sheds light on the inherent dichotomy between what teachers understand about the meaning and purpose of education and the implications of what they do with the rest of their time in a mediated world in meaningful ways.

John Henry Cardinal Newman said in his *Idea of a University* (1854) that all true knowledge is purposeful when it is active and the student critically relates existing knowledge and experience with new knowledge to come to new understandings. Stephanie Flores-Koulish presents the educational community with a valid work that acknowledges the media world as school and encourages the educational academic community to regard media literacy education with eyes wide open.

Rose Pacatte
Director, Pauline Center for Media Studies

Chapter One

Why Must Teacher Education Care About the Media?

The average U.S. citizen spends 9.2 hours each day engaged in media information/entertainment (V. S. & Associates, 1999). This level of media exposure has created a powerful influence within our lives, one that far exceeds and is vastly different from the democratic values being taught in many schools (Bartolome & Macedo, 1997; Gerbner, 1995; Giroux, 1994). But television and other one-way media (i.e., the Internet is a two-way media) generally do not allow for engagement or dialogue, an important component of a democracy. It is rare then that we can even question the media to which we are exposed so much. And while most of us have the capacity to ask questions of the media we are exposed to, if only to question ourselves rhetorically, does this happen naturally or do we purposefully "turn off" our thinking when we encounter certain media texts? Most likely the answer lies somewhere in between these poles. However, the ability to question the media requires a deeper knowledge base of media aesthetics (that would vary depending on the medium), media history, and other socio-cultural and political issues underlying media production and content.

Media literacy education is a critical tool that we can use to experience the media differently with democratic and even liberatory implications. Media literacy education is defined as "the ability to access, analyze, evaluate and communicate messages in a variety of forms" (Aufderheide, 1993). Ideally, access means that we can seek out a variety of sources from various mediums (e.g., television, Internet, newspapers, etc.) when it comes to a particular news story, for example. Then, we analyze and evaluate to "read" and make judgments about the media we experience. And by communicating with a variety of media, we can become better "readers" by understanding how production decisions might be made.

Media literacy education has yet to spread widely within the U.S. education system. Like other social movements, media literacy is primarily "fed at the grass-roots level by classroom teachers, not by centralized bureaucracies" (Considine, 2000a). However, a large number of U.S. centralized bureaucracies (or officials in state education departments) have heeded the call for this skill base and validated media literacy education by including it to varying extents within the curriculum frameworks of 48 states (Kubey & Baker, 1999). But within the NCATE[1] standards for elementary preservice teacher education programs, there is very little, if any, mention directly of media literacy education for undergraduate elementary education majors. This is compounded by the lack of academic literature within teacher education on this topic. Therefore, there appears to be a disconnect between what budding teachers learn and the expectations and explicitness expressed by the states in setting standards for their future students. Given the above, part of the problem I investigated was whether preservice teachers are prepared to teach media literacy as mandated in these frameworks. Specifically, I wanted to discern just what kind of knowledge, skills, beliefs, and experience preservice elementary teachers have in place in relation to the requirements for elementary students. To do so, I turned to the current media-related curriculum frameworks developed by the Commonwealth of Massachusetts.

A necessary consequence of my investigation into preservice teachers' knowledge and experiences of media literacy was also a look into this group's general "media world"; that is, I investigated a group of preservice elementary teachers who volunteered for this study. It was important to discover their perceptions of the media and their exposure to various media, in the past and in the present. Len Masterman (1986) writes, "The media are important shapers of our perceptions and ideas. They are Consciousness Industries which provide not simply information about the world, but ways of seeing and understanding it" (p. 3–4). And so it is important for teacher educators to look beyond the state mandates to know how future teachers make sense of media information/entertainment. This will provide useful information for teacher educators to better understand their students' lived experiences. At present, we do not know much about this particular group's awareness and/or the lenses by which they experience the media world. In fact, Rosenbaum and Beentjes (2001) found that in general "little research has been concerned with measuring so-called entry behavior; i.e., knowledge of the media that pupils possess before entering a media education project" (p. 468). Therefore, this study attempts to fill a gap in the research literature.

PURPOSE OF THE STUDY/RESEARCH QUESTIONS

The purpose of this study is multidimensional, for it was based on Lee Shulman's concept of content knowledge for teachers (1989). It involved my investigating the knowledge, skills, beliefs, and experiences preservice teachers have in relation to the media literacy and the teaching of it. (I elaborate on Shulman in the next chapter.) I initially wished to uncover the prior knowledge that undergraduate preservice elementary schoolteachers had regarding media literacy education. While I did not expect the preservice teachers to be aware of the term "media literacy education," I had hoped to learn to what extent they were familiar with its elements. Next, I wanted to comprehend their own media literacy skills as well as how they might consider teaching it. To what extent were they able to employ media literacy skills either for themselves and/or for others? And finally, I intended to find out what experiences these future teachers have had with media literacy, whether on a personal or professional level and/or in a formal learning/teaching capacity. And again, as a natural and useful by-product of this investigation, I discovered aspects of these participants' personal lives in relation to media information/entertainment.

All of this will lead to better elucidation of their overall skills, knowledge, and in particular, their beliefs in relation to the media, popular culture, and media literacy education. In her 1996 article, "The role of attitudes and beliefs in learning to teach," Virginia Richardson expanded on and emphasized the importance of teachers' knowledge and beliefs. First she distinguished between the two by determining that teacher knowledge has been operationalized in a way as to compare it with instinctual actions by an experienced teacher. She writes, "it is personalized, idiosyncratic, and contextual and, for Yinger (1989) emerges during action" (p. 104). On the other hand, she defines beliefs more generally as "a proposition that is accepted as true by the individual holding the belief" (p. 104). There is thus a symbiotic relationship between the two with each playing a significant role in a teacher's actions. "Beliefs are thought to drive actions; however, experiences and reflection on action may lead to changes in and/or additions to beliefs" (p. 104). This is important in this particular study whereby the media and the way we are exposed to them may shape our beliefs. Thus, asking preservice teachers to pause and reflect on their knowledge, skills and beliefs of the media and popular culture are helpful not only for their individual development in media studies but also for their growing pedagogical content knowledge. And as Richardson summarizes, "within a constructivist learning and teaching framework . . . beliefs should be surfaced and acknowledged during the teacher education program if the program is to make a difference in the deep structure of knowledge and beliefs held by the students" (p. 106). Another dimension of this study provides suggestions for delving into the knowledge and beliefs of preservice teachers regarding the media and media literacy education.

To address these complex issues, this study pursued the following questions:

1. What is the range of media that these preservice teachers have experienced in the past and currently? What media do they prefer?
2. How do preservice teachers analyze and evaluate various media? How have they learned to do this?
3. How do preservice teachers understand the aesthetics of media?
4. To what extent have preservice teachers designed and created their own media?
5. To what extent are preservice teachers aware of media literacy?
6. How prepared are preservice teachers to teach media literacy?

DEFINITION OF TERMS

Media literacy and media education are essentially synonymous expressions. Media education is the preferred phrase used in other English-speaking nations, and I often combine the two terms, calling it media literacy education. It is also important that I stress that media literacy education is not exclusively content, but also a skill. David Considine (2000) writes, "media literacy constitutes both a subject of study and a method or process of teaching." Media literacy calls for the study of popular cultural texts, but it is also a way to examine more than the latest popular film. For example, media literacy scholar Renee Hobbs (1998) suggests the following 5 questions be asked of all media messages:

1. Who is sending this message and why?
2. What techniques are used to attract my attention?
3. What lifestyles, values and points of view are represented in the message?
4. How might different people understand this message differently from me?
5. What is omitted from this message?

These key questions then provide a model of inquiry to students for investigating an array of institutional messages. In the next chapter I highlight and distinguish among the media literacy research, but it is important to note here that my particular focus lies more closely within a cultural studies framework such as Carmen Luke (1998) describes:

> Although cultural studies remains primarily in the theoretical custody of men, it is, like feminism, concerned with the *specificity* of reading positions and cultural productions on the one hand and, on the other, concerned with the politics of power/knowledge regimes in the media(ted) construction of identities and knowledge. (p. 23)

In this work I will use the terminology media, popular culture, and media information/entertainment nearly interchangeably. My intention is to include a variety of means by which our culture and/or news is transmitted, either to very large audiences ("mass" media) or through personal media (the Internet). In addition, most of the media I refer to is one-way; it is created by someone (or some people) to be "read" by others (the audience). However, this is not an exclusive unidirectional flow when referring to the Internet, because the Web can include authorship by its "readers." Media, as I intend, are also not exclusively visual either, but can be a combination of various visuals with music, spoken or printed words. And, depending on the specific medium (i.e., film, television, etc.), visuals, music, and words, for instance, are treated differently by the authors for varying desired effects. The media texts I will refer to include television shows, films, advertisements (on the mediums of TV, billboards, and magazines, to name a few), Websites, magazine articles and photographs, and "popular" music.

Regarding the frameworks of the US states I referred to, Kubey and Baker (1999) used the following operational definition of media literacy in their assessment of the state documents: "A state framework was judged to call for media education only where use, analysis, evaluation, or production of electronic media other than print was included, or where the word 'viewing' was specifically used" (p. 2). In chapter two I elaborate on the state frameworks and media literacy.

ASSUMPTIONS

The majority of early communication research studies examined the media through behaviorist lenses. "Theorists argued that propaganda messages were like magic bullets that could easily and instantly penetrate even the strongest defenses. No one was safe from their power to convert" (Baran & Davis, 1995, p. 71). Audiences were believed to be passive sponges that soaked in and believed all of the messages created by the media. According to John Fiske (1994), "This discursive construction of the audience as the disempowered empty receptacle waiting for the message underlies . . . the whole tradition of effects research" (p. 196). Research in mass communication has evolved paradigmatically since the early 20th century, but recent research still implies that we are never really capable of full cognitive awareness when it comes to the media (Barry, 1997). With much of this type of hard science behind media reception, how is it that I wish to push forth a field such as media literacy, which, according to the research above, may not deliver on its promises of cognitive awareness? According to Hodge and Tripp (1986), there is validity for such a field if it approaches the study of media and meaning with sophistication and complexity. That is, "research into TV must . . . treat [social understanding] as an integral part of a viewer's normal experience, as but one of a large number of complexly interacting aspects of our culture which both defines and is defined by other parts within the whole." Essentially, I assume that while we may never be fully aware of all media messages, with media literacy skills we can become savvier in our media choices, and in general, in the depth to which we experience media texts. Additionally, if we are truly media literate, we would then be able to create and find outlets for alternative media voices, which can only enhance notions of democracy. My assumption here may be aligned with the authors of the state frameworks, and perhaps some in teacher education also agree, yet we are left to question why there is not a greater presence of media literacy in teacher education.

A second assumption in approaching this study was that while I knew I might have been surprised at the level of analysis the participants displayed during this study, I did not expect them to be highly sophisticated in their depth of knowledge of media literacy. Philosopher Douglas Kellner writes:

> It has been my experience in over twenty-five years of teaching that students and others are not naturally media literate, or critical of their culture, and should be provided with methods and tools of critique to empower them against the manipulative force of existing society and culture . . . (p. 60).

This assumption comes with the conjecture that they had not had any media literacy instruction in their school careers. So while I did not expect a deep level of media analysis from the participants, I assumed that they would have some abilities to detect elements of media manipulation because they have grown up so immersed in media texts.

LIMITATIONS

The greatest conceptual limitation of this study is that I am attempting in the upcoming pages to explain with text an issue that is not about text. But since it is still an emerging field, perhaps as media literacy expands, researchers will begin to present studies such as this through multimedia. In other words, instead of creating narrative descriptions of the various video texts watched during the research process, a hypertext link from a multi-media presentation might take the "reader" into the environment in a way that would be similar to how the participants experienced it.

Additionally, this study only includes data of preservice *elementary* teachers, and not secondary majors. Why is this? Because the absence of re-search on media literacy in elementary education is greater than in second-ary education. This could be due in part to the nature of single-subject curriculum and the depth content must reach at the secondary level. That is, secondary teachers must cover their subjects more deeply and therefore there is room for media analysis. Additionally, it is often put forth that teenagers are favorite targets of the media and therefore the most suscepti-ble to media influence (assuming this is usually negative). While I do not en-dorse the assumption that media literacy is only important to overcome negative media influence, I feel that media analysis needs to begin at an ear-lier age, so that young people grow up learning how to "read" visuals and multimedia messages. In terms of this study, I assume that fewer elementary education teachers have the "skills" themselves to "read" the media, and thus to teach about it.

PERSONAL SIGNIFICANCE

> Writing that infuses the blood and bones of the writer's life with what she or he is writing reconceptualizes the purpose of art. Therefore, as I struggle with the tensions created by my own contradictory practice of writing that includes personal stories, I ask for your indulgence and, perhaps, even for your acceptance of writing that blends public and private forms—understanding that acceptance of a nontraditional form of writing, in this instance, is also counterhegemonic because it questions textual authority and patriarchal tradition (Brunner, 1994, p. xv).

As an elder member of "Generation X," my "coming-of-age" story is all about media. Broadcast options increased during my adolescence, and television became the messenger for the majority of my information. I clearly recall visiting *Fantasy Island* every Friday night after taking a tour on *The Love Boat,* and of course, I yearned to be in a family like *The Brady Bunch.* In other words, I grew up watching and enjoying television a lot, and movies became a necessary social activity.

Expanding media options also provided texture for my "coming of age" with the advent of such things as VCRs, cable television, video games, and compact discs. The stylistically influential institution that is Music Television (MTV) began in 1981, when I was in high school, along with CNN's 24-hour news coverage. As a young adult, I befriended someone who had attended film school, and with his shared knowledge, my aesthetic appreciation of media increased, which led me to dabble in my own video productions. I did not experience computers until I was 20, but with that as the end of my early media experiences, it should show the deepened media exposure of those younger than I am—in particular, today's preservice teachers.

"The nature of our pleasures, particularly the pleasures we gain from our relationships with the media, needs scrutiny as well as celebration" (Ferguson, 2000). While I grew up pleasurably engaged with popular media and created my own media, I have realized that it is also important to examine the media's messages critically. This is important because many of the messages that are being brought to us serve various purposes and influence our lives. Media literacy provides a model through which consumers can discover various purposes behind the media we experience, and thus make more informed media and personal choices. It is for this reason that this study, which expands research in media literacy to teacher education and thus helps propel this burgeoning field, is of significance.

OVERVIEW

This study presents two major findings within the overall field of media literacy education. First, I provide a sketch of the knowledge, skills, beliefs, and experiences of a group of preservice elementary teachers in relation to the media, popular culture and Shulman's elements of content knowledge. Second, based on the findings above, information from the literature on media literacy and literature in teacher education, I have suggested a conceptual model, which can be helpful for future related policy, practice, and research for teacher educators and those working with teachers in the field of media literacy education.

CHAPTER ORGANIZATION

The book contains seven chapters. Following this chapter, chapter two aids in placing this research study among other related research in media literacy. I review three bodies of literature: (a) the emerging issues from the research on media literacy education; (b) media literacy and the U.S. standards movement; and (c) media literacy and the needed content knowledge. In chapter three I describe the particular methods and methodologies I utilized to conduct this qualitative study, as well as how I analyzed data and proceeded with my findings. Chapter four provides an in-depth contextual view of the participants and the time we spent in the discussion groups. This is appropriate background for the following two chapters, which elaborate on the various themes that emerged from my analysis of the survey, in-depth interviews and discussion groups in relation to Shulman's three areas of content knowledge (see Figure 1).

In chapter five—entitled "Preservice teachers and media/popular culture"—I focus on Shulman's area of content knowledge, subject matter knowledge in relation to media literacy. In chapter six, entitled "Preservice teachers' knowledge and teaching of media literacy," I examine and highlight aspects of the two other areas of content knowledge, pedagogical and curricular knowledge and abilities. Coming out of all of this in chapter seven, I reemphasize the profile of these particular preservice teachers, but perhaps more importantly provide a conceptual model and implications for future related policy, practice, and research.

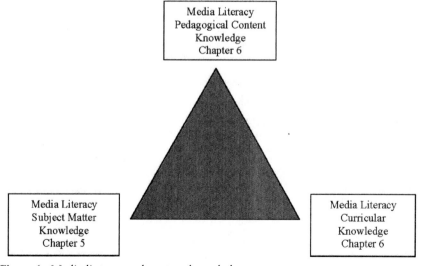

Figure 1. Media literacy and content knowledge

Chapter Two
Setting the Context

MEDIA LITERACY: THE BACKGROUND

Reviewing the literature in media literacy education requires a wide purview of varying disciplines. This is true because media literacy education is a field in its infancy within the United States with advocacy roots that are spread thinly among various fields. It is not a topic that emerged from legal mandates, nor is it an area that has come about as a result of a "grand theory." Rather, some would say that it is a field that has grown consequently from the expanding notions of literacy in our evolving information age. Concerned parents, educators, academics, health professionals, politicians, and many other groups have noticed the gap between the entertainment industry along with the information superhighway led by business professionals and the literacy content and pedagogy in today's schools. Still others in these groups are concerned about media content and what they believe are negative influences on youth culture. With these forces emerging, it is clear that schools can no longer afford to limit education to print literacy skills. There are deep, nuanced messages contained within the visual, aural, and sensual arrangements of the ubiquitous media that surround students, teachers and society. Some in these groups have determined that media literacy is the best response to these phenomena. One researcher defines media literacy as "the ability to access, analyze, evaluate, and communicate messages in a variety of forms" (Aufderheide, 1993).

My analysis here examines five aspects that emerged from the literature on media literacy. In the first section, *Media Literacy in the United Kingdom*, I chronicle how media education began from a range of beliefs, fields, and practices there. The second section, *Media Literacy in the United States: The Media Literacy Movement* expands from the first section to describe how it is popularly theorized and practiced in classrooms here. The third section, *Media Literacy in the United States: Critical Pedagogues* elaborates on a more overtly political media literacy, which generally sits on the margins. Naturally expanding from these three sections is the fourth that examines, *Why Incorporating Media Literacy Is Important, Yet Problematic (in the United States)*. Media literacy has been included in the new curriculum frameworks in most states, but little teaching or true understanding of it as a field exists for various reasons that I will highlight. As a result of this small presence, it is also problematic that very little research exists on what happens when teachers try to introduce media literacy to their students. The final section, *Media Literacy and Empirical Research*, further discusses this.

MEDIA LITERACY IN THE UNITED KINGDOM

In the field of media literacy, Britain has led the world in theory and practice. According to University of London education professor David Buckingham (1998), "In comparison with the U.S., media education in Britain has a much longer history and is more firmly established within the school curriculum" (p. 33). As the title to his article, "Media Education In The UK: Moving Beyond Protectionism," implies, the media literacy movement in the United Kingdom has moved beyond its original mid-20th century grounding in protectionism or inoculation for children against media's potential or inevitable harm. Its beginnings could be seen as a reaction against early Hollywood, which some felt was a type of moral corruption (Masterman, 1985). The literature of Buckingham and Len Masterman, another leading British media education scholar, provides a history of theoretical grounding that is useful for U.S. scholars as we try to advance the movement here.

Masterman (1993) writes, "if the media were a definite kind of cultural disease, then media education was [originally] designed to provide protection *against* it" (p. 6). One could say protectionists had as their slogan "just say no" to media. This original theoretical grounding was displaced in the late 1950s and early 1960s by a film appreciation canonical slant, called the *popular arts* approach, which differed from the previous one rather dramatically. Instead of looking at media texts as debasing and demoralizing, connoisseurs emerged who judged one text as better than another. Once again, however, educators realized that the popular arts method was too limiting and exclusive in terms of the media texts it included. For this reason, Masterman advanced the *screen education* perspective. This approach looked to apply "a number of structuralist ideas, particularly in the areas of semiotics and ideology" (p. 8) to practical classroom use. In the area of semiotics, questions of representation were brought up in relationship to the media. In semiotics, one would ask if the media really represent reality or do they just construct multimedia to appear real? Questions of value were confronted that directly opposed the previous two approaches.

In his 1998 introduction to *Teaching Popular Culture*, Buckingham explains media education in the United Kingdom, historically and currently, as a dichotomous negotiation between differing approaches. First, he places Masterman as the leader of an approach that seeks to use semiotics to analyze media texts broadly "to reveal their suppressed ideological function. Teaching about the media thus becomes a process of demystification, of revealing underlying truths, which are normally hidden from view" (Buckingham, 1998, p. 8). Buckingham sees the other impulse led by those who characterize popular culture "as an authentic part of students' experience, hence as something which teachers should seek to validate and even celebrate" (p. 8). Studying this negotiation carefully can be helpful for media literacy proponents in the U.S. as we advance in this field.

MEDIA LITERACY IN THE UNITED STATES: THE MEDIA LITERACY MOVEMENT

A review of the literature in this category does not produce much, because despite the fact that it now has a "curricular foothold" in most of the framework documents in the United States (Kubey & Baker, 1999), it has yet to spread into schools very widely. Thus, there is not a large amount of literature. With what little information is available, this section concentrates on the more "mainstream" approaches that have emerged in our country to address media literacy, also known as the liberal pragmatist conceptualization (Anderson, 2002). Many of the academics and educators I place in this section have come from communication departments, where the study of media is already a major portion of the curriculum. Still others define themselves as media "activists."

A hub of the movement in the United States has been the Center for Media Literacy in Los Angeles, more media activist than academic. It began as a magazine *(Media and Values)* in 1977 led by Sister Elizabeth Thoman, a Roman Catholic nun, but later it was "'reinvented' and renamed in January 1994 as the Center for Media Literacy, [and] the organization began to focus more on national leadership, resource distribution, and teacher training for the emerging U.S. media literacy movement" (CML, 2000, para. 3).

Much of the Center for Media Literacy's inventory of U.S. material is of a mainstream nature; in other words, few of the authors take extreme ideological positions when it comes to media analysis, and few are teacher education professionals. David Considine is one worth mentioning, however. He is a faculty member at Appalachia State University in Boone, North Carolina, which is "the largest teacher training institute in the tenth-largest state" (Considine, 1997, p. 246). According to Considine (1997), the university requires all undergraduate preservice teachers "to take one course that addresses the subject of media literacy and its role in North Carolina's curriculum" (p. 246). In addition to undergraduates receiving media literacy in this course, the faculty works together to blend elements of traditional teacher education curricula with media literacy competencies.

Considine is on the board of directors of the new national organization called American Media Literacy Association (AMLA). Perhaps the following e-mail message he sent in to a media literacy listserv describes his more pragmatic approach:

> Two areas where I find school administrators, teachers, PTO's (parent teacher organizations), media specialists and so on receptive to this wider approach are 1. Responsible citizenship for a democratic society and 2. Productive and skilled workers. One advantage of such a strategy as I have argued from many, many years of experience, is that it aligns media literacy WITHIN the mission statement of schools, rather than asking them to accept yet another innovation. (Considine, 2000b)

Clearly Considine, along with another popular figure in the movement, Renee Hobbs, is working within existing structures and systems to introduce expanded notions of literacy competency. Additionally, Considine and Hobbs are less likely to declare media literacy education as a political action.

Hobbs is a communications professor at Temple University. Like Considine, she has worked hard to promote media literacy among teachers, but her work has mostly encompassed in-service teacher instruction and curriculum writing. An important contribution she recently made to the advancement of media literacy was her article, "Literacy for the information age," which appeared as the first article in the *Handbook of Research on Teaching Literacy Through the Communicative and Visual Arts* (Flood, Brice Heath, & Lapp, 1997). The article describes the key components of media literacy and discusses the power and importance of its integration into schools (Hobbs, 1997a). The key components Hobbs lists are:

1.   All messages are constructions.
2.   Messages are representations of social reality.
3.   Individuals negotiate meaning by interacting with messages.
4.   Messages have economic, political, social and aesthetic purposes.
5.   Each form of communication has unique characteristics (p. 9).

And while Hobbs suggests that to be media literate one should consider political purposes of messages, she is still passive in her beliefs that media literacy is "radical pedagogy" or a political act altogether. Thus individual responsibility supersedes a concern for collective, community involvement. Anderson writes, "I see [this group] believing that by creating a particular type of mental faculty in a student the ability to 'think for themselves' a teacher is creating the potential for change without necessarily directing the spirit of that change" (Anderson, 2002). In other words, there is an underlying political tenor to this field, but "mainstream" proponents seem to avoid this admission.

MEDIA LITERACY IN THE UNITED STATES: THE CRITICAL PEDAGOGUES

Many would argue that Paulo Freire is perhaps the greatest influence on many critical thinkers and writers in education today. In his book, *Education for Critical Consciousness,* he presents a foundation for educators to promote dialogic learning for individual empowerment and community liberation, which should lead to "just" social reconstruction (Freire, 1973). Some believe this is a major task for media literacy educators since the media are such an enormous hegemonic teaching force, which many claim far exceeds classroom instruction (Bartolome & Macedo, 1997; Giroux, 1994). Critical pedagogue Henry Giroux has written about critical media literacy in various places (Giroux, 1992, 1994). In his book, *Disturbing Pleasures* (1994), he further sets up justification for critical media literacy:

> Moreover, the shift in the political toward popular practices has made clear that the hybridized space of popular culture is where the conflicts over the related issues of memory, identity, and representation are being most intensely fought over as part of a broader attempt by dominant groups to secure cultural hegemony. (p. 27)

Freire, Giroux, Lilia Bartolome, and Donaldo Macedo (1997) set up strong justification for taking action in terms of the media. David Sholle and Stan Denski (1995) offer a definition: "Being media literate means both having a voice, and giving the other a voice—seeing one's subjectivity in the threat of the other and then overcoming that threat in the recognition of the partiality of one's own perspective" (p. 27). Critical pedagogues suggest that the process of critical media literacy is conducted through constant questioning (Hammer, 1995; Tyner, 1998) ideally leading to social reconstruction.

While it seems as though the basis for proponents of critical media literacy is one of alarm, in fact, it can be a more moderated approach. Rhonda Hammer (1995) writes:

> Once students are able to enjoy a program, while still being analytical, they can begin to translate these critical insights into other kinds of learning and expression (and eventually, we hope, into their own counter-hegemonic media productions). Through this process they come to learn not to be deceived by 'absolute' answers, nor by absolute relativity; they recognize the importance of constantly asking questions. (p. 36)

This statement echoes the optimistic philosophy of scholars such as the pragmatist Cornell West, who writes, "If you look in a text and see yourself, that is market education, done in the name of education. But education must not be about a cathartic quest for identity. It must foster credible sensibilities for an active critical citizenry" (1993, p. 217). Thus, action becomes a key outcome of this particular approach.

Critical literacy/reading scholars such as Donna Alvermann and Margaret Hagood promote media literacy education by stating that "literacy is on the verge of reinventing itself" (p. 193). They write about the 1995 presidential speech at the 43rd annual meeting of the National Reading Conference, in which James Flood expanded the notions of literacy beyond the printed word, and specifically urged "incorporating critical media literacy in school curricula" (p. 203). They define critical media literacy as follows:

> [It] may be characterized as the ability to reflect on the pleasures derived from mass media and popular culture practices (e.g., radio, TV, video, movies, CDs, the Internet, gang graffiti, and cyberpunk culture); the ability to choose selectively among popular culture icons; or the ability to produce one's own multimedia texts (Alvermann & Hagood, 2000, p. 194).

Scholars in the field of reading just may be the magnetic force for bringing media literacy education to teacher education.

Many of the scholars mentioned here are more theoreticians than curriculum and instruction practitioners, which is perhaps why critical media literacy has not entered into the teacher education curriculum more frequently. Buckingham (1998) agrees and expands:

> Originating in a neo-marxist analysis this work has increasingly taken on the identity politics of gender and ethnicity, and has sought to incorporate the insights of a wide range of new theoretical perspectives,

including postmodernism, poststructuralism and postcolonial theory.
(Buckingham, 1998, p. 6).

However, he also explains that much of this critical work is not grounded
within classroom realities. That is, Giroux, McLaren and others write, without the voices of students in their work. Additionally, within their theoretical perspective they have received criticism from others, namely feminist
scholars, who

> have challenged the way in which "critical pedagogy" seeks to incorpo-
> rate quite distinct political and theoretical projects into a single overar-
> ching synthesis–or what feminists have termed its "master discourse"
> . . . their texts are replete with injunctions about what teachers should
> do, but entirely devoid of suggestions about *how* they should do it.
> (Buckingham, 1998, p. 7).

Further, Weaver and Daspit (1999) find that these critical approaches can be
constraining due to their limitation on multiple readings of media texts.
They suggest that teachers should "decenter" their readings:

> By decentering we do not mean the abandonment of emancipatory agen-
> das, ethical imperatives, or radical democratic projects. It does mean,
> however, that critical theory drops any notion that these goals be under-
> girded by what the radical postmodern feminist Wendy Brown calls po-
> litical entailments or an epistemological assumption that implies our
> political agenda guarantees progress or liberation. (p. xix)

In other words, teachers should be open to co-discovering with students pro-
gressive interpretive actions of media texts.

And so it seems in the United States as well as abroad that stances toward media literacy pedagogy are developing and based on an array of ideological understandings from audience reception and media effects research to
fundamental views of the purpose of education. In the next section I develop
an explanation of the challenges to including media literacy in education.

WHY INCORPORATING MEDIA LITERACY IS
IMPORTANT, YET PROBLEMATIC

The differing underlying levels of criticality as previously outlined are but a
glimpse of the many divisive fragments that perhaps prevent media literacy
from expansion in the U.S. public school system. There are many controver-
sies surrounding and within it. To refocus the divisions above, there is a
struggle over whether media literacy should have a more explicit political

and ideological agenda (Hobbs, 1998). According to Hobbs (1998), "to the dismay of radical educators, media literacy concepts and instructional practices are attractive to people with a wide spectrum of political beliefs" (p. 23). She goes on to say: "There is an obvious ideology that underlies even the most basic tenets of media literacy education—teaching students to question textual authority and to use reasoning to reach autonomous decisions" (p.23). So it seems obvious that no media literacy proponents are denying the political nature of this content, but some eager advocates are wary, at this time, of pushing a critical ideology perhaps for fear of continued neglect in the current neoconservative U.S. environment. Therefore, members of the "mainstream" organization promote a "critical thinking" paradigm for individual sophistication, while critical pedagogues remain steadfast and aim at larger collective social reconstruction. And together they splinter attempts to create legitimation as a new field of study.

I believe the fragmentation has been further perpetuated by the recent creation of yet another national media literacy group. It is called ACME (Action Coalition for Media Education). ACME has similar goals as AMLA; that is, helping people become media literate. But additionally, ACME members are quite zealous in their pursuit of reform of the media itself. They believe that "activists have made considerable headway in promoting democratic values, challenging censorship, fighting for equality and confronting corporate interests in the media" (ACME, 2003, paragraph 2), and thus they staunchly reject any and all large corporate connections. Instead, they are committed to thrive as independent and at the grassroots.

Another roadblock, located at the school level, is the dramatic rise in in-school commercialism. The General Accounting Office of Congress recently released a report on this growing phenomenon in which businesses offer cash-strapped schools equipment and supplies in exchange for the students as captive audiences for advertisements (Hays, 2000). This is a problematic area for media literacy because, while in-school advertising is a "natural" curriculum for students to critique, its mere presence in schools has the opposite effect of consumer celebration. More specifically, some media literacy experts can suggest that teachers make use of this corporate material in order to critique and question its message and/or purpose without a problem. But once these same experts combine with the corporations to create an official media literacy curriculum, the integrity of the field is at risk. This, in fact, happened when Hobbs wrote a media literacy curriculum unit for Channel One[1], and the Partnership for Media Literacy (organizers of the annual conference) accepted conference sponsorship from the controversial corporation. Some would say this issue strongly contributed to the creation of ACME.

In discussing the current economic boom globally and the accountability society we live in today, Michael Apple (2000) provides further obstacles to the integration of media literacy in school curriculum. According to Apple, what is at work is a combination of "the neoliberal market and the regulatory state, (which) . . . on the one hand this makes a socially and culturally critical pedagogy even more essential, (but) it also makes it much more difficult to accomplish" (p.248). Thus, we are left with the question: Can media literacy, whether overtly political or not, realistically thrive in the United States without at times co-opting with sympathetic, opportunistic corporations and/or governmental directives? This rhetorical question can only be answered by the gradually shifting tides of our economic existence and postmodern realities.

MEDIA LITERACY AND EMPIRICAL RESEARCH

Roger Desmond (1997) speaks quite firmly of the need for "hard data on effectiveness [of media literacy] from the research community" (p. 29), which touches on the last aspect of media literacy: the dearth of empirical research. Ann Sweet, at the Office of Educational Research and Improvement (OERI), wrote in 1997 that, "although there is growing sentiment among educators for the integration of literacy and the visual/communicative arts, a comprehensive search of the literature produced very few empirical studies conducted on this topic during the past decade" (p.271). Rutgers communications scholar Robert Kubey (1998) confirms this and offers two suggestions. First, he sees the need for more research that will enable educators to understand what children already know about the media. Second, he calls for research in terms of its efficacy, or whether media literacy's critical skills can be transferred to other domains. My study, while not focusing on children per se, should effectively contribute to Kubey's first claim.

My study adds to a third area where research in media literacy education is needed: in preservice teacher education. That is, if we know that students in 48 out of the 50 states need to know varying aspects of media literacy, we certainly need to know if new teachers are media literate and prepared to teach it. In her theoretical piece entitled "Literacy expanded: The role of media literacy in teacher education," Gretchen Schwarz (2001) makes a case for its inclusion in teacher education methods, cultural foundations and psychology courses. She writes:

> Teachers who are critical thinkers and good communicators, who challenge the status quo when needed, who are both skilled and thoughtful in the uses of technology across disciplines, who understand their own

culture and others—are teachers who can help their students achieve the
same goals in their own lives. (p. 118)

Beyond this important justification, however, my exploration has uncovered
very little empirical research of media literacy education within teacher
preparation programs in the United States (Considine, 2000a; Gathercoal,
2000). The research that does exist involves limited but useful surveys and
small case studies (Hamot, Shiveley, & Vanfossen, 1998; Luke, 2000;
Ottaviani, 1997). Therefore, my study can begin to contribute to this needed
body of knowledge.

MEDIA LITERACY AND STATE FRAMEWORKS

The fallout after the publication of *A Nation at Risk* in 1983 put a spotlight
on public schools, and the entire field of education became a hotbed of critique leading to rigid requirements and "clear" expectations, generally referred to as "standards," or in some state's cases, "frameworks," which
culminated in the federal law entitled *No Child Left Behind*. Initially, some
opponents were worried that frameworks would just be a list for a "back to
basics" approach, but scholars and educators within the media literacy
movement particularly, have shown otherwise. Kathleen Tyner, in her book,
Literacy in a Digital World (1998) writes,

> Media education, with its reformist pedagogies, close relationship to
> emerging communication forms, and goals toward strengthening demo-
> cratic structures, is in a central position to support educational reform
> that is responsive to learners and in harmony with the world outside the
> classroom (p. 228).

Luckily, writers of frameworks in 48 states seem to agree, but what history
lies behind this bureaucratic advancement of media literacy? And how do
particular states, namely Texas, Minnesota, and Massachusetts, define the
term and its expectations? (I am choosing these three states for their exem-
plary design and breadth of media literacy standards as discussed by authors
I refer to in this section, and I am focusing on Massachusetts specifically to
relate to my particular study.)

The history of the recent standards movement is a short one, and in
turn so is the history of the inclusion of media literacy education standards
in the United States. It is important to note, however, that the United States
is last in terms of including media literacy standards in education. Kubey
and Baker (1999) write, "since the mid-1990s, Australian language teachers
have been required to teach nonprint media from kindergarten through the

12th grade. The Canadian province of Ontario has required media education in grades 7–12 since 1987." They also write of the bureaucratic advances of media education in England, Scotland, and South Africa.

In the United States it seems that we can trace the development of state standards in media literacy to parts of the national standards of such organizations as the National Council for Teachers of English-International Reading Association (NCTE-IRA), the National Communication Association (NCA), the American Association of School Librarians, and the Association for Educational Communications and Technology ("both of the American Library Association") (Goulden, 1998; Lacy, 2000). In a 1998 presentation to the NCA, Nancy Rost Goulden mentioned the NCTE-IRA's bold moves away from an exclusive reliance on printed text and composition toward a focus that also includes "viewing . . . graphics, and technological communications," or nonprint media and technology.

Tyner also investigated the NCA standards, and she lists them.

The goal of the standards is to ensure that the "effective media participant can demonstrate":

1. the effects of the various types of electronic audio and visual media, including television, radio, the telephone, the Internet, computers, electronic conferencing, and film, on media consumers; and
2. the ability to identify and use skills necessary for competent participation in communication across various types of electronic audio and visual media (p. 203).

However, in her presentation Goulden also reported that the NCTE-IRA wrote, "ideally, teachers, parents, administrators, and students will use (their standards) as starting points for an ongoing discussion about classroom activities and curricula" (p. 4). Therefore, while these national organizations' standards must have served as useful guideposts for the authors of the various state frameworks, it is unclear to what extent they were actually influential. In fact, in Lyn Lacy's contribution to *Reconceptualizing Literacy in the Media Age* entitled, "Integrating standards in K-5 literacy," she gives her account of how she participated in the creation of media literacy standards for the Minneapolis Public Schools within the Information and Media Technology (IMT) Content Standards. She wrote, "the preface to these standards defines media literacy as 'the ability to access, analyze, evaluate, and produce communication in a variety of forms'" (p. 236). While Lacy, an elementary media specialist, refers to the various national standards in her article, she also provides details of her personal teaching experiences with non-print media analysis and production that she has had since the late 1970s, reaffirming Considine's (2000) premise that media literacy has generally emerged from grassroots efforts.

Tyner (1998) writes that the Minneapolis Public Schools' IMT strand is "unique in standards development at the K-12 level because they blend media analysis and practice with information technology in a newly conceived, yet mandated, area of the curriculum that makes the need for media and technology education explicit" (p. 219). However, Tyner, as well as Kubey and Baker, offer Texas the most applause. Kubey and Baker write, "overall, we concluded that Texas unquestionably presents the most developed and comprehensive media education framework." Specifically, media literacy is embedded as viewing/representing/interpretation, analysis, and production within English Language Arts. Additionally, however, it is included within the social studies and health strands, and as well, there is a "stand-alone elective for media literacy in a Speech/Communication strand" (Tyner, 1998, p. 204) within the English Language Arts and Reading standards.

Since my study focuses on teachers going through preservice teacher education in the Commonwealth of Massachusetts, it is important to elaborate specifically on the media literacy standards there. First, it is important to explain that the standards for media literacy are not included across disciplines, as in some other states (as Texas' are explained above). However, unlike some other states, there is a separate strand for media in Massachusetts, which is within the English Language Arts area, and these standards are intended for students in grades PreK through 12. Goulden (1998) praises the writers of the Massachusetts frameworks for their consistency "with NCA recommendations for understanding the influence of the media itself" (p. 12).

The three standards are:

1. Students will obtain information by using a variety of media and evaluate the quality of material they obtain.
2. Students will explain how the techniques used in electronic media modify traditional forms of discourse for different aesthetic and rhetorical purposes.
3. Students will design and create coherent media productions with a clear controlling idea, adequate detail, and appropriate consideration of audience, purpose, and medium (*Massachusetts Curriculum Framework: English Language Arts,* 1997).

Clearly the writers of these standards had the formal definition of media literacy in mind, as access and evaluation correspond to the first standard, analysis is a large part of the second one, and communication (or production) is expected in the third.

In addition to the three standards above, there are also detailed expectations laid out for grades PreK through 4, 5 through 8, 9 and 10, and 11 and 12 respectively. For example, in the first strand, the standard for PreK through 4 states that the students will "use electronic media for research." For the second standard, these same students should be able to "identify techniques used in television and use their knowledge to distinguish between facts and misleading information." And lastly, that same group should be able to "create age-appropriate media productions (radio script, television play, audiotape, etc.) for display or transmission." The designers of this document also included concrete examples for each standard and grade range.

MEDIA LITERACY EDUCATION AND TEACHER CONTENT KNOWLEDGE

A few years ago, while I was teaching high school, I wanted to do a small unit on violence in the media with my freshman English class. The unit's structure became a content analysis (Manning & Cullum-Swan, 1994) research format, in which I asked each student to choose a television show and record the number of acts of violence in the program. Together we operationalized our own definition of television violence as all physical and verbal harm against another person or animal. And we agreed on parameters of the project. The students were to watch one television show and identify and record the number of violent acts. They were to report their findings to the class in an oral presentation (corresponding with their formal curriculum), which was left rather loose in terms of the format, but they had to have some sort of visual representation. On one of our presentation days, a student asked me if he could show the selection he had videotaped from television. In my teaching naiveté, I agreed enthusiastically without previewing it first.

The student's example came from MTV and was called *Celebrity Death Match*. I had never seen this program and knew nothing about it, but given its title and the nature of our project, I knew it contained violent content, but I also thought that because it came from MTV, it would not be too graphic for this age group. My initial enthusiasm quickly turned to anxiety, however, as I listened to the class laughter when claymation characters began, literally, to tear each other apart in an animated boxing ring. But since I had said they could view this one example, and I did not want to be disrespectful toward their viewing choices, I allowed the program to go on for nearly 15 minutes. Then I facilitated the continuation of their presentations as if we had simply seen a poster with hash marks displaying someone's benign data. It was one of those regrettable teaching moments when the giggling students know they "pulled one over on the teacher."

Upon reflection, I knew I could have done more, because this particular show was deeper than I described above. The two characters that were fighting were claymation representations of the real-life film directors, Spike Lee and Quentin Tarantino, both of whom have utilized elements of violence (and sex) practically as trademarks in their work. One is black, the other white. Both are young and controversial. The choice of these two characters in a duel to the end was high sarcasm and wit, as was the accompanying dialogue. While I was watching the program in the class that day, I intuitively understood and enjoyed that level of humor. My students, on the other hand, laughed when someone's head fell off. I could have capitalized on that beautiful moment and we could have discussed these layers, but at the time I did not have the pedagogical content knowledge for how to proceed, and their sole appreciation for the surface content matter stunned me. So instead, the opportunity became one of the most awkward moments of my teaching career, perhaps fueling me further to pursue my current field of media literacy education.

Before this teaching experience, I knew a little about media studies, but the content I had learned did not include *how* to teach it. Given the fact that elements of media literacy, again defined as "the ability to access, analyze, evaluate and communicate media in a variety of forms" (Aufderheide, 1993), are included in 48 out of 50 states' frameworks (Kubey & Baker, 1999), it should be imperative that teachers know how to teach it. The challenge however, is that media change at a rapid pace; therefore, my argument in this section, using the literature, is that teachers need the enduring pedagogical skills to teach and discuss with their students new media texts as they are released. Teacher education can help with this process. Within teacher education, media literacy can include an array of content knowledge for teaching, consisting of subject matter knowledge, pedagogical content knowledge and curricular knowledge. I will explain each of these, as well as provide examples of published accounts of its current inclusion in a few teacher education programs, thus leading to further support for the inclusion of media literacy education in teacher education.

While there are not many scholars calling for the inclusion of media literacy in teacher education, there are some (Brown, 2001; Cortes, 2000; Cox, 1993; Gathercoal, 2000; Langrehr, 1997; Tyner, 1998). In his 2000 presentation at "Summit 2000: Children, youth and the media beyond the millennium," teacher educator Paul Gathercoal showed how difficult it is for us to separate ourselves from the ubiquitous media:

Since the commercial media define much of the educator's world, it is difficult for educators to know how to address the media. Teachers have never been taught how to "teach the media." Largely media education is ignored because no one has addressed it in the past and so many educators think it must be something that parents and caregivers need to address in the home. Media studies programs are necessary for developing in students the knowledge, skills and dispositions needed to be responsible citizens in a free society (p. 4).

In a study published in 1998, researchers Gregory E. Hamot, James M. Shiveley and Phillip J. Van Fossen used, as their foundation, the same claim as Gathercoal: "The preparation of future social studies teachers to teach the relation between mass media and effective democratic citizenship is the focus of the present study" (p. 241). They surveyed secondary social studies teacher educators in Ohio and found that while a majority defined media understanding as "technical acuity *and* critical thinking," (p. 248), only a minority included it within their courses. Their findings suggest that while these particular teacher educators generally saw the connection between the media and social studies education, most have generally yet to include it within their syllabi. Perhaps this absence of media studies in social studies teacher education is due to the fact that even teacher educators have lacked the needed skills.

Clearly the need is present. At a 1993 annual discussion of the National Council of Teachers of English (NCTE), Carole Cox, then the director of the Commission on Media, claimed that "several areas of continuing concern persist. . . . Teacher education programs should include media literacy" (p. 11). A separate paper could be written on why this has not yet happened. However, since that is not my current focus, I will simply provide one conjecture. Gathercoal (2000) seems to believe that it has to do with the infusion of technology education. He wrote:

The United States Department of Education has expended millions of dollars to help preservice teachers to be better prepared to use technology in teaching. For many teacher preparation programs this means using computers and not critically reading the messages they provide. These initiatives take precedence over any hope of preparing preservice teachers to teach about the media and their messages (p. 4).

In other words, as with the fundamental tenets of *No Child Left Behind*, content and product are favored over process or pedagogy.

We must also remind ourselves that teacher education needs more than a media or communication course. In her article entitled "Communication education: Pedagogical content knowledge needed," Cassandra Book (1989) wrote, "faculty in the areas of mathematics education, science education, writing, and reading have examined questions about the teaching and learning in their particular subject areas. What characterizes these faculty is that they know well their subject area as well as pedagogy" (p. 315). Teacher education is the place where content is fused with pedagogy; therefore, media literacy education needs to be there. Gathercoal illustrated this need further:

> In the United States, when Media studies is taught at all, schools commonly teach about specific media content and call this practice the "teaching of media literacy." . . . In other words . . . schools are teaching content and not process. A reading analogy would be that students are acquiring a wonderful "sight word" vocabulary, but they are unable to "sound out" words they have not been taught to read. With the changing nature of commercial media messages, this type of curriculum is about as useful as learning "dead languages" (p. 4).

What teachers need then is a variety of content knowledge with respect to media literacy education. Book wrote, "How teachers understand the disciplinary knowledge and how they represent that content to students through the individual pedagogical content decisions and the broader curricular decisions they make affects the nature of knowledge students will come to have about the discipline" (p. 320). What are the different types of content knowledge that a teacher needs? Lee Shulman answered this question in terms of general knowledge for teachers in his 1986 article, "Those Who Understand: Knowledge Growth in Teaching." He wrote, "I suggest we distinguish among three categories of content knowledge: (a) subject matter content knowledge, (b) pedagogical content knowledge, and (c) curricular knowledge" (p. 9). The following discussion is based on Shulman's definitions of each area.

First, Shulman (1986) explained that subject matter content knowledge "refers to the amount and organization of knowledge per se in the mind of the teacher" (p. 9). Book (1989) emphasized this area for communication education with a plea that teachers understand the history of the discipline, as well as have a clear understanding of its inherent importance and applicability. Perhaps the latter part of Shulman's definition is most important in terms of teaching, for teachers must have a mental representation of content in order to present it effectively to different types of learners. In a study with preservice physical education teachers, Inez Rovegno (1992) found that "content knowledge acquired in other times and places was initially used at a general, undifferentiated level, and became redifferentiated in the new setting in terms of the goals of helping children learn" (p. 78). In other words, it is important for a teacher to be able to access her wider understanding and schemata of a topic to know how to challenge a variety of students. Perhaps in my case from the opening story, it may have helped if my familiarity with *Celebrity Death Match*, the two directors, and/or comic devices had been stronger. That would have enabled me at least to redifferentiate and facilitate a discussion on the various aspects of knowledge present during this teachable moment.

In terms of media literacy education within teacher education, some teacher education programs do provide the subject matter content knowledge by asking preservice teachers to access, analyze, evaluate, and communicate media in a variety of forms (e.g. Considine, 2000; Luke, 2000; Ottaviani, 1997; Semali, 1993). In her 1997 paper, Barbara Fields Ottaviani explained her personal motivation for including media literacy content within a teacher education technology class. She wrote, "to produce media-literate students, elementary educators must have a clear understanding not only of how multimedia interactive technologies can enhance learning events in their classrooms, but they must also be aware of the underlying issues associated with children and television" (p. 93). Education students at Appalachia State University gain production skills, but David Considine (2000) writes, "They also look deeply at what it means to be literate in a media age" (p. 315). At Pennsylvania State University, teacher education professor Ladislaus Semali teaches a course in media literacy where education students "recognize, read, comprehend and question ideas and information whether conveyed through print or picture; [and they learn to] critically analyze, and evaluate media messages for simplification, distortion, bias, and propaganda" (1993, p. 219). Media literacy content knowledge thus enables teachers to gain the skills for viewing media differently themselves, which is important developmentally for any content.

Media literacy in Australia is more evolved than in the United States, and correspondingly, so is its presence in teacher education. Literacy professor Carmen Luke describes a course in New Literacies at the University of Queensland:

> The course is organised around the concept of multiliteracies (New London Group, 1996). . . . The concept begins with the assumption that people confront and negotiate the everyday world using a diversity of literacies with which to decode the multiple and densely layered environment of symbolic and iconic, cultural and social semiotic meaning systems (p. 429).

This course begins with a history of communication media and the university students learn about the "influence of, for instance, hieroglyphics, the alphabet, the printing press, the telephone, and the Internet on social organisation, learning, teaching, knowledge, and power" (p. 429). By including an emphasis on power, Luke's critical pedagogical approach would meld nicely into various teacher education programs in the United States for which critical pedagogy is a focus.

The next area of content knowledge that Shulman defines, pedagogical content knowledge (PCK), is what some education scholars emphasize distinguishes and validates the importance of education programs for teachers (Berliner, 2000). Shulman writes that PCK

> goes beyond knowledge of subject matter per se to the dimension of subject matter knowledge for teaching. I still speak of content knowledge here, but of the particular form of content knowledge that embodies the aspects of content most germane to its teachability. . . . In a word, the ways of representing and formulating the subject that make it comprehensible to others (p. 9).

He explained further in 1987 that this area of knowledge is what differentiates "the understanding of the content specialist from that of the pedagogue" (p. 8). This is also a basis for the argument supporting teacher education for all teachers, and in this case, it supports the inclusion of media literacy education specifically in teacher education.

Since Shulman advanced these ideas about PCK, others have written on and expanded his ideas. In particular, Kathryn Cochran, James DeRuiter, and Richard King (1993) called for teachers to have pedagogical content "knowing" (PCKing):

> In this expanded version of PCK, we place increased emphasis on knowing and understanding as active processes and on the simultaneous development of all aspects of knowing how to teach. In our version of PCK we emphasize the importance of teachers' knowing about the learning of their students and the environmental context in which learning and teaching occur (p. 263).

They explained that their ideas for pedagogical content knowing are based in constructivist ideas of teaching where knowledge is "actively created by the knower and not passively received in an unmodified form from the environment" (p. 265). This expanded version of PCK corresponds with more recent reception theories in communication (Hodge & Tripp, 1986), and therefore it is appropriate for media literacy education. That is, as Cochran,

DeRuiter, and King explain PCKing, knowledge creation and media reception are similarly complex tasks involving consideration for broader cognitive and sociocultural elements.

Fortunately, much of the structure of media literacy contains pedagogy within it. That is, part of doing media literacy involves asking fundamental questions about media and society. Corresponding with PCKing above, Dan Langrehr (1997) wrote that

> [D]ecoding media through analysis and evaluation in a classroom environment can align teachers and students as collaborators in up-to-date research. Both teachers and students become co-investigators of mass media influence; they analyze and synthesize the text and mode of this information (p. 5).

This was what I attempted with the high school freshmen by asking them to conduct a content analysis of a television show with acts of violence as the individual units. At Appalachia State University, education students are taught about Instructional Conversations (ICs) which are like threaded conversations that encourage dialogue and questioning (Considine, 2000). Considine wrote, "the class comes to understand ICs not as abstract theory, but as classroom practice. It is the type of practice inherent in the belief that audiences negotiate meaning" (p. 316), corresponding with PCKing. In keeping with many current pedagogical theories, media literacy in classrooms is "fresh and relevant classroom dialectic applied to dissect and decode mass media influences" (Langrehr, 1997, p. 6). Perhaps it was skillful dialogic facilitation then that I lacked in my earlier teaching.

An additional component of media literacy education in teacher education should include teachers recollecting their personal media histories, but for a specific purpose. Some people may have extensive knowledge of media from personal consumption, yet having this deep knowledge is not enough. Suzanne Wilson, Lee Shulman, and Anna Richert found that "in studying novice teachers, it is clear to us that teachers need more than a personal understanding of the subject matter they are expected to teach" (1987, p. 104). However, personal knowledge can and should be a validated and useful foundation. In this case, perhaps tapping into future teachers' media histories can reveal various perceptions and/or misconceptions about the field of teaching, which could then be compared and contrasted with personal experiences.

In general though, personal knowledge of a subject alone has been found to be insufficient for teaching success. In her study of physical education majors, Rovegno (1992) found that "even when content knowledge acquired from the perspective of a learner/athlete was strong, there is evidence that this knowledge was not differentiated enough in terms of teaching and how children learn and did not support generating appropriate feedback" (p. 76). Further, Pamela Grossman, in her book *The Making of a Teacher: Teacher Knowledge and Teacher Education* (1990), described a comparative case study of six novice teachers, three of whom went through teacher education and three who did not, but did major in the content area. The particpants who majored in the subject area in college based their pedagogy on personal undergraduate classroom experiences and thus faced difficult challenges in the classroom. The three teacher education majors utilized the theories of pedagogy they learned in their education coursework for more classroom success. What Grossman found were "troublesome implications" in assuming that content knowledge and classroom experience were sufficient for new teachers (p. 141). This is a problem in relation to media literacy education as well given its dearth within teacher education.

Another important piece of Grossman's book in relation to media biography is that "many of teachers' ideas of how to teach particular topics can be traced back to their memories of how their own teachers approached these topics" (p. 10). Therefore, recollecting and reflecting during teacher education on one's previous classroom experiences should be paramount so as not to replicate "bad" teaching, which has been documented in terms of classroom media use.

Media usage in classrooms has been found to be not so democratic and participatory. Renee Hobbs discovered that teachers misuse media in classrooms in ways such as turning on a video and then grading papers or "awarding" a video after the students have behaved well. This type of media practice in classrooms promotes the passive consumption of media (Hobbs, 1993; Hobbs, 1997), and sadly, it is the type of media usage in classrooms many of us have experienced. Cassandra Book describes PCK in such a way that teachers would transform their knowledge bases given their personal preconceptions and/or experiences about content (Book, 1989). In their article, "Education: The Overcoming of Experience," Margret Buchman and John Schwille (1983) argue that, contrary to popular belief, experience is not the best "teacher." They claim that it may instead prevent us from freely choosing alternatives, because these alternatives might contrast with what we see and do firsthand. They continue by arguing that either theory, or secondhand information, is more valuable because it can be reflected upon and critiqued before implementation. Teaching media literacy education in teacher education then would enable preservice teachers to go beyond their firsthand experiences of media usage, whether personally and/or from their prior classroom experiences.

The third area of Shulman's content knowledge for teachers is curricular knowledge:

> The curriculum is represented by the full range of programs designed for the teaching of particular subjects and topics at a given level, the variety of instructional materials available in relation to those programs, and the set of characteristics that serve as both the indications and contraindications for the use of particular curriculum or program materials in particular circumstances. [This is curricular knowledge.] (Shulman, 1986, p. 10)

For Cochran, et al., consideration of "environment" in PCKing can encompass this area of content knowledge. It would be important for teachers to know where they can obtain the most appropriate and wide array of curriculum for their particular students. Once again, a course in media literacy education could facilitate this.

A course in media literacy during teacher education preparation could point preservice teachers in the direction of where to find the available resources. Paul Gathercoal (2000) agreed that this third component is equally important, "Teacher preparation programs need to . . . provide teachers with the expertise and knowledge of resources to implement Media studies programs in schools" (p. 4). Dan Langrehr (1997) described a PBS program called *Media Literacy: The New Basic* (1996), that "offered inquisitive educators access routes to media literacy strategies through study guides, curricula materials, video cassettes, and websites" (p. 7). While the availability of published curricula is sparse, there are various resources available in the United States for teachers such as listservs, websites, curriculum packages, and videos.

Without the help of teacher education, advancing media literacy education continues to be a great challenge. In her study of physical education teachers, Rovegno found that a particular methodology within physical education was marginalized, but once the preservice teachers learned this they "situated their commitment to the approach as being part of a social mission bigger than themselves" (Rovegno, 1993). Preservice teachers, therefore, need only to be introduced to media literacy and I believe they will become proponents. I know if I had had instruction in the challenging skill of fostering dialogue in relation to the media, I would not have found myself so stumped by *Celebrity Death Match*. And so it could begin with teacher educators who have power to help facilitate the growth of media literacy education in the United States. Hopefully, more will begin to act soon.

Chapter Three
Design of the Study

PURPOSE

The purpose of my study was multidimensional. First, I intended to find out what sorts of experiences undergraduate elementary education majors have had with media literacy, whether on a personal or professional level and/or in a teaching capacity. As a natural and useful by-product of this investigation, I also discovered aspects of these participants' personal lives in relation to media as information and as entertainment, both at home and in their schooling. Next, I uncovered the prior knowledge that these undergraduates have had regarding media literacy education. Finally, I realized the skills they have in relation to teaching or doing media literacy. By doing media literacy, I am referring to a personal skill. I sought to learn, then, the extent to which the participants were able to employ media literacy skills and conceptual understanding either for themselves and/or for others. So to discover this rich descriptive information from a particular group of preservice teachers, qualitative methods best suited my pursuit.

In this chapter, I begin by describing my research design, which includes the methods and perspectives that informed this research. Following this, I explain the general research questions that guided my process. Next, I briefly describe the participants, and then I illustrate the data collection process. I follow that section with a description of my particular methods of data analysis and interpretation. Since I, as a qualitative researcher, am the instrument (Lincoln & Guba, 1985), I also elaborate briefly on the role of the researcher in this study. I end with two brief sections detailing various ethical issues as well as the possible methodological limitations and strengths involved in this study.

RESEARCH QUESTIONS AND DESIGN

To gain an understanding of the knowledge, skills, beliefs, and experience that undergraduate elementary education majors have regarding media and media literacy, I utilized methods and perspectives from naturalistic inquiry, grounded theory, and critical ethnography. As is imperative to naturalistic inquiry, I was the instrument within this study, which was built on my "tacit knowledge" of media literacy using qualitative tools (Lincoln & Guba, 1985) such as surveys, in-depth interviews and discussion groups. This methodological triangulation (Patton, 1990) thus strengthened my study. I am familiar with various issues in popular culture, and the field of media literacy, and as I describe below, I also understand aspects of Massachusetts education, all of which undoubtedly have informed this process yet remained more or less at the tacit level during the data collection.

Grounded theory perspectives added to my study in that I simultaneously collected data and analyzed them (Charmaz, 1995). This perspective enabled me to create the form of my data collection as I proceeded through the process. Specifically, for the first individual interviews, I created a protocol based on an analysis of the survey data (which I explain in more detail below). During the data collection sessions, I used audiotapes for recording purposes, but I did not generally take notes while I was engaged in questioning and observing. Instead, each time I returned home after a session, I wrote notes in a journal, which helped me to think through and analyze the process as it unfolded. These notes also later served as memos or "analytic notes to explicate and fill out categories" at a later date (Charmaz, 1995, p. 28).

Knowing that there is a dearth of research in media literacy education and teacher education, I approached my study in a way that sought to discover "what could be," which is a goal of critical ethnography (Thomas, 1993). In other words, in pursuing this study I wished to increase its appearance in the education field, which is clearly a political purpose. Thus it is in sync with the aims of critical ethnography:

> Conventional ethnographers generally speak *for* their subjects, usually to an audience of other researchers. Critical ethnographers, by contrast, accept an added research task of raising their voice to speak *to* an audience *on behalf* of their subjects as a means of empowering them by giving more authority to the subjects' voice. (Thomas, 1993, p. 4)

When I initially asked the five subgroup participants why they were interested in volunteering for my study, their answers were resounding in terms of their desire to know more about a field that they felt was very important for teachers to understand. In the upcoming pages I speak on their behalf to acknowledge not only their desires to know more but also their awareness of how much their past education, from elementary school through their teacher education programs, featured or lacked media literacy education. Even the larger objective of having preservice teachers become proficient in media literacy education exists so that future generations will have a chance to become media literate as well. And with its "strategies that blend critical literacy, experiential education, and critical pedagogy" (Tyner, 1998, p. 230), it is very much in line with critical ethnography's "emancipatory goals [which work] to negate the repressive influences that lead to unnecessary social domination of all groups" (Thomas, 1993, p. 4).

After establishing my methodological orientation and considering the larger field of media literacy education, I created the following research questions, here divided into major categories:

Media Consumption

- What is the range of media that these preservice teachers have experienced in the past? What media do they currently experience? What media do they prefer?

Media Subject Matter Knowledge

- How do preservice teachers analyze and evaluate various media? How have they learned to do this?
- How do preservice teachers understand the aesthetics of the media?
- To what extent have preservice teachers designed and created their own media?

Media Literacy: Pedagogical Knowledge

- To what extent are preservice teachers aware of "media literacy?"
- How prepared are they to teach media literacy?

PARTICIPANTS: A BRIEF INTRODUCTION

I gained permission through the formal human subjects review from two higher education institutions to study a group of their undergraduate preservice teachers in the elementary education major. Both institutions are located in Massachusetts, but each is quite different from the other. One school is a large private university in an urban area and has a separate school of education; the other, a small liberal arts college in the suburbs, has a small education department.

I limited the study to the geographical proximity of Massachusetts because of my familiarity with this state's education system, both as a teacher and as a doctoral student of education. In my five years as a resident and educator, I experienced firsthand the infusion of new education initiatives by this state in relation to standardized curriculum frameworks and high-stakes testing for students and teachers. Each of these also played a factor in my research. Specifically, I have seen firsthand and through the media how a high stakes teacher test has affected various education departments/schools. These effects relate to my research in that an underlying purpose (Thomas, 1993) of my study is to try to provide data which will help to build future teacher education curriculum. However, if a state test determines a person's teaching eligibility, schools of education might become wary of new material outside the domains of the test. In fact, I counter this potential argument in the previous chapter, where I analyzed the Massachusetts frameworks that call for media literacy education. However, I have yet to find media literacy education included in the state test, MCAS, nor have I found it within Massachusetts teacher education.

The primary reason I chose these two particular institutions, beyond their differences, was for access purposes—so I could connect in person with potential participants at the start of the study. I had contacts at each school; thus, I introduced my project in person to four education classes and asked for the participants' volunteer participation in an on-line survey. I gave a brief background of who I was and what my study involved. I gave participants the Website address for the survey and explained that it should take only about 10 minutes of their time. I also told them that there were two other phases after this initial one for which I was also seeking volunteers and that they could contact me via electronic mail if they could assist. Within the web-based survey, I included a paragraph (see appendix A) that reiterated my search for a subgroup of volunteers, which included my contact information.

Twenty-five participants completed the survey out of a potential group of one hundred, and five volunteers contacted me for the next phase. Within two weeks, I began the first round of individual interviews with those five volunteer participants. Let me digress here briefly and explain that the human subjects review process was held up at one of the institutions, and therefore I did not receive permission until near the end of the participants' spring semester. For this reason, my data collection was concentrated within a short period of time, as I had to conduct all four of the discussion groups while the preservice teachers were all still in the geographic area. This is important to acknowledge, for it speaks to the level of commitment by the sub-group participants, especially the three graduating seniors, and it also begins to describe our process as one that was intense as opposed to spread out over a significant period of time.

Besides three graduating seniors, two other participants who were finishing their freshman year volunteered to be in the subgroup. All of the participants were white and female, though their socio-economic and regional background varied somewhat. However, they were all from the Northeast. (In chapter 4, I provide a detailed description of each subgroup participant.) As the final phase of my research, I conducted the second interviews at their homes (except for one), which gave me a greater sense of their varied socio-economic and cultural situations. Thus, while diverse economically, the group was quite appropriate as a "homogenous sample," which Patton (1990) describes as optimal for group interviews.

DATA SOURCES/COLLECTION

The three data collection methods I used included a descriptive survey, two in-depth interviews with each subgroup participant, and four "discussion groups," all of which appear in Table 1 on the following page, and which I describe in detail below.

To establish a basic grounding and gain a general descriptive sense of the answers to the large questions I wanted to ask in my study, a survey seemed a most appropriate way to start. However, after a lengthy investigation I discovered that such an instrument for preservice teachers and media/media literacy did not exist. Therefore, I designed my own, which went through collegial review and subsequent iterations. Upon creating what seemed to be a final draft, to establish a sense of validity, I asked a random group of about 10 to take the survey and comment. The survey appeared in electronic form through the Web service, Websurveyor.com. Since I just wanted basic descriptive results, this service was appropriate and helpful, for it provided me with not only a design template but it also allowed me to access my results in report form using pie charts or bar graphs see Appendix A.

Upon examining and questioning the survey results, I created a narrower list of questions I wished to pursue further for the first in-depth interviews (see Appendix B) with the five subgroup volunteers who also took the survey. These questions ranged from ones of a biographical nature to various opinion/value-oriented questions (Patton, 1990) about the media, popular culture, schooling and media literacy. And while the interviews technically could be classified as "standardized open-ended interviews" (Patton, 1990),

Table 1.

Data Collection—Spring 2001	
PHASE ONE—25 PARTICIPANTS	
Method	Description
Websurveyor.com	41 Questions
PHASE TWO—5 PARTICIPANTS	
Method	Description
Individual in-depth interviews	Approximately 1 hour
Discussion Group 1	Approximately 2 hours
	Open-ended questions
	Viewed Madonna's music video
	Viewed "House Hippos" video
Discussion Group 2	Approximately 2 hours
	Discussed Case A & B
Discussion Group 3	Approximately 2 hours
	Viewed media literacy video *Signal to Noise*
Discussion Group 4	Approximately 2 hours
	Perused media literacy Website
	Built media literacy standards for teachers/students
Individual in-depth interviews	Approximately 1 hour

I allowed them to take a casual conversational form. In other words, while I followed a similar scheme for each participant, when there was a particular area that seemed interesting and relevant to me, I pursued it with probing questions. I also followed my feminist methodological sensibilities by sharing various aspects of myself that seemed to coincide with their own stories (Harding, 1987).

Patton writes that focus groups are interviews and not discussions or "problem-solving session[s]" (Patton, 1990, p.335). While some may classify my next method as a "focus group" given the nature of my chosen theoretical tradition, that term was not appropriate, as I purposefully aimed for these groups to be problem-solving sessions. To learn about their social nature with the media, in these group meetings I wanted the participants to share their media experiences and opinions with each other, both from their schooling and at home. I wanted to get the participants' reactions to children's media. I wanted to see what they thought about media literacy and its available curriculum. In short, I chose to use the term "discussion group" for these sessions, which lasted 2 hours including a meal break where I paid to get food delivered.

My overall design for the four sessions operated from the inside out. In discussion group one, I began by again asking the same five participants I interviewed a new set of questions (see Appendix C) after I examined and queried the interviews I had transcribed verbatim, in order to dig more deeply. After this, we watched a controversial music video by the popular musical performer, Madonna, for her song, "What It Feels Like for a Girl." My intention was to choose a piece of media that was somewhat meaningful to their worlds, and in the interviews, I hoped to learn of a particular piece of media in which they shared in enjoyment. Much to my surprise, there was no overlap. For this reason and keeping in mind the sanctity of time, I chose to have them view a music video. This particular Madonna video had recently received media attention for its controversial nature. MTV showed it once at a late hour with disclaimers. Its content was quite similar to the story line in the film, *Thelma and Louise*. That is, its theme is about women reclaiming, through force and violence, all that they have lost as a result of male hegemony. Given this description, I assumed that viewing it would generate the rich discussion that follows in the upcoming pages.

Following the music video on the same tape was a "cute" Canadian public service announcement that hinted at what media literacy is: the act of questioning the media. It accomplished this with computer graphics portraying a miniature hippopotamus living in someone's house ("House Hippo") with documentary-style narration describing this unusual animal. At the very end of the 30-second piece, the camera pulls out to reveal a real hippopotamus in its natural environment and a different announcer saying, "That looked really real. But you knew it couldn't be true, didn't you? That's why it's good to think about what you're watching on TV and ask questions." Up to this point, I had asked them in the survey and during the first interview to define media literacy, and I could tell their grasp of the concept was tenuous. This short video gave them a highlight of its meaning. After viewing both segments, we had an open-ended discussion on each.

For the second discussion group meeting, I wanted to move away from their media worlds and step into children's media with the intent to understand how the participants might discuss children's media, but I also took the opportunity to see how they might build curricula using children's media. To do this I designed two cases. Case A centered on a first grade teacher's assignment that I designed. In this "make believe" assignment, the teacher told the students to go home and watch a "science show" with their parents, record three facts and bring them to school the next week. In our discussion group after I explained this much, I distributed cue cards for each of the participants to read aloud what five students had brought in as facts. The fifth cue card, however (I numbered each card to be read in order), said that this student brought in his example and wanted to show it to the class. At that point, the subgroup and I watched an episode of the children's cartoon, *Dexter's Lab*. I chose this particular cartoon after asking my two nephews, who are 7 and 10, what the most popular shows are for kids their age. They told me about five shows, mostly cartoons, which I taped and previewed. I decided on *Dexter's Lab* because it fell in conjunction with the mock assignment by the first grade teacher.

It is important here to digress briefly and describe the cartoon we watched. *Dexter's Lab* is about a boy named Dexter who has a laboratory in his house. In this particular episode, the teacher gives his class an assignment for a "show and tell" project. Immediately, Dexter's classmate and "arch rival" stares at him, implying a competition. They each have a "super" pet they want to bring in for show and tell, but after each gives his pet a potion, the pets destroy the boys' home laboratories and by the time they come into class, both pets are sound asleep.

After we watched the cartoon we discussed the scenario as if they were the first grade teacher. I asked the participants if they would have allowed the class to watch the cartoon, which led to an open-ended pedagogical conversation. Following this discussion, for Case B, I distributed five class sets of media surveys (see Appendix D) that had been recently completed by sixth graders in an upper-middle-class suburban middle school (I obtained the surveys from a language arts teacher). Each participant received one class set, and I simply asked them to review the surveys. While the audiotape ran, the participants expressed with each other their various opinions about the sixth graders' media preferences. No questions were necessary as the conversation flowed naturally. From there I gave the participants two basic lesson plan templates, and I asked them to create, as a group, two lessons for these students based on the sixth graders' media preferences.

For the third discussion group we watched the video *Signal to Noise: Life with Television*, which is a PBS-produced video that contains a series of short videos by independent filmmakers who created pieces that analyze various aspects of TV. Some of the shorts have the flavor of independent films' spirit in that they take a tongue-in-cheek sort of look at television. Essentially, the short videos analyze the social influence television has had within various segments of our society and our society writ large. I chose this particular media literacy video after submitting a question to "media-l," a media literacy electronic mailing list to which many prominent professionals in media literacy belong. I simply asked the list members to recommend a powerful media literacy video for undergraduates. Twelve videos were recommended (17 people responded), and *Signal to Noise* received the most votes.

Prior to viewing the video, I gave my participants work sheets with a basic set of questions (see Appendix E) that we read out loud, and afterward, they used these questions to guide their conversation (the work sheets had spaces, in which some of them jotted notes). This method minimized my interjections.

In the final discussion group we focused more specifically on "media literacy," particularly media literacy curricula. We did this by my asking the participants to carefully review a Website that contains numerous links for media literacy education, from ready-made teaching units to "critical" articles to resource catalogs. This Website is housed at the University of Oregon and is regularly updated (http://interact.uoregon.edu/medialit/MLR/home/index.html). The participants explored the site for 45 minutes, and again, I gave them a work sheet (see Appendix F). This time I simply asked them to jot down notes on anything in particular that interested them and that they might revisit in the future.

For our final activity as a group I asked the participants to create a set of standards on media literacy for elementary and teacher education students. As their last task, which fell during final exam week for one of the schools, they seemed to have "lost steam." This is not to say that they did not complete this part, nor should it imply that their product was "bad." I simply feel it is important to acknowledge the fact that while they did show effort at this task, it was not with the same fervor that I had seen.

I interviewed the participants a final time individually (see Appendix G for interview protocol). I felt this provided my study with a bookend-like structure, or pre- and post-assessment if you will. This time I traveled to the participants' homes for the interviews (except for one who was still in the area), which took place one month after the last discussion group. I began the interviews, as I had begun most of the discussion groups, by asking the participants if they had thought about and/or discussed media literacy since the last time we had met, and if so, I asked them to share their thoughts. Again, I built my interview protocol based on my analysis of all the data, which I had transcribed verbatim, up to that point in time. I asked all the participants a core set of questions, but I also asked specific questions of individuals based on my analysis. That is, I probed deeper into certain areas that seemed to me as valuable from their words on the tapes/transcripts.

DATA ANALYSIS

A significant part of my analysis took place during the data collection, as per grounded theory. The survey became the foundation of the data analysis from which questions emerged for the initial interviews and first discussion group. As I moved through the data collection process, I transcribed the sessions on the same day that I conducted the various interviews, and I then probed deeper into significant areas to ask more questions for richer responses. In the research journal I kept, I also wrote notes in the manner of the "constant comparative method" (Glaser & Strauss, 1967) by comparing the responses within and among the participants. After the data collection I then conducted a general "cross-interview analysis" (Patton, 1990) using the hard copies of my transcripts. I read the transcripts numerous times and made notes in the margins and elsewhere. I also reviewed the various analytical field notes I had taken. From all of this I came up with a list of a 45 codes that emerged from the data, again as per grounded theory (Charmaz, 1995). I applied the codes to the data using the qualitative software, HyperResearch. HyperResearch is a tool that enables a researcher not only to code data but also to access it in various forms through the generation of reports. I chose to generate reports for each of my codes across the transcripts. This exercise provided me with chunks of text for each code and enabled me to re-read my data in a new form, which helped build the framework of the story that I shall illustrate in the following chapters. In other words, I collapsed the 45 codes together in a way that moved from the literal to the theoretical in which themes emerged around these participants' media backgrounds, as well as within the teaching of media literacy. Throughout this process, I also "talked through" the evolution of this analysis with various colleagues who helped me to ask myself and my data "large" questions to constantly justify the larger and even more important academic question, "So what?" This led to my overall argument: These preservice teachers in the undergraduate elementary education major have an interest in deepening their knowledge of media literacy; however, they are lacking in terms of their content knowledge (Shulman, 1986), which could be remedied with the inclusion of media literacy education in preservice teacher education.

MY POSITION

Only one of the participants knew me before I began this project, and she only knew of me, barely, as a colleague. While there were no issues of my being their supervisor or teacher, as is the case frequently in educational research, my title as a Ph.D. student, I felt, carried with it "baggage." That is, I noticed at times (both live and after transcribing) that the participants asked questions of me as if I were their teacher. For example, they asked, "Is that what you're looking for?" I did not give this consideration until after the final discussion group, but in the last interview I began by bringing up this issue directly. I told them I had noticed this discourse from the transcripts, and I reminded them that I was a researcher, not a teacher. I told them that meant I wanted them to express their thoughts freely; not try to give a "right" answer. While the discussion groups appeared to be like a class, my involvement, beyond asking questions at times, was minimal and unlike a teacher.

ETHICAL ISSUES

As per the human subjects review process at my university, I took care to treat my research participants in an ethical manner. For the survey, all responses came to me anonymously. And each member of the subgroup of participants chose their own pseudonyms. Each of these participants also agreed to participate by signing a letter of consent (see Appendix H). Beyond these requirements, however, I chose to offer the subgroup a monetary incentive for their participation. After all the data collection was completed, I mailed each participant a letter of appreciation (see Appendix I) along with a check and a packet of media literacy resources. I should also add here that, given my personality, I always viewed my participants as just that, "participants" and not "subjects." For this reason, I found myself still in contact with them periodically long after the data collection had ended. Specifically, I sent them various media literacy resources following the U.S. tragedy on September 11, 2001.

METHODOLOGICAL LIMITATIONS AND STRENGTHS

As with most studies, various methodological limitations occur, and thus merit listing. Perhaps the most glaring limitation of my study was its concentrated nature. I think that if I had been able to spread out the interviews and various discussion group sessions over a longer period of time, the data may have been richer. Some may say, however, that it may not have been "better," only different. With more time perhaps these participants would have had more of an opportunity to reflect upon all the information in a deeper way. Additionally, perhaps what I discussed earlier in terms of their interpretation of my position also skewed some of the data prior to the final interview. In other words, because it seemed that some of them viewed me as an authority figure (i.e., a teacher), I am left to wonder how this affected their responses. Perhaps another limitation of my study had to do with my knowledge base and/or assumptions of media literacy. How did my particular subjectivity, as an aspiring expert in the field of media literacy, affect my duties as a researcher?

Some might believe that my background and particular interest in media/media literacy, popular culture, and teaching provided me with strengths that might elude others pursuing similar research. That helped me to relate to many of the things my participants shared. But additionally, I have fortunately been exposed to the field of media literacy and teaching, and therefore, I have a particular understanding of what it takes to translate this content into pedagogy, and how to access its curriculum. This provides me with a level of trustworthiness in terms of the judgments that I apply within my analysis of the data. Considering each of these issues individually and collectively is important to recollect while reading what lies ahead.

Chapter Four
The Participants and Our Discussions: An In-Depth Portrait

This chapter lays down a foundation by describing the participants in detail beyond the information I provided in chapter three, and as well richly illustrates the discussion groups from which much of the analysis that appears in the ensuing chapters emerged. The major purpose of this chapter then is mainly to provide a biographical familiarization with the individual subgroup participants, with an emphasis on the media, popular culture, and schooling. Additionally, I provide a vivid retelling of what transpired during the four discussion groups in which we delved into the many nuances of the media and popular culture in relation to their personal worlds, teaching, children and our culture in general.

The first section of this chapter provides a general description of all the participants in the study with emphases on demographics along with a brief comment on why the five subgroup participants chose to participate further in the study. Following that description is a more detailed, individualized portrait of each of the five participants in relation to the media and popular culture. The next section of this chapter includes further explicit narration of my observations from the bulk of the data collection, concentrating specifically on the four discussion groups, leaving rich quotes and analysis for later chapters. All of these descriptions combined, again, allow for a deeper understanding of the context from which the analysis emerged for the upcoming chapters.

THE PARTICIPANTS, IN-DEPTH

In my research I found no similar studies that have been published on preservice teachers' beliefs, etc., regarding the media. It is important to note, however, that I do not assert that my data are generalizable beyond the sample in this study. I am stating that claim here to emphasize the fact that the five preservice teachers who participated in phase two of my study were all white women. That is, while I am not focusing on issues of race directly in this study, this point is important because without mentioning it I would be perpetuating age-old presumptions of whiteness as colorlessness. It is common knowledge that white females are by far the majority in elementary teaching across the United States, and so this should not be overlooked as less than a particular factor within my research. In many ways, this factor actually strengthens my study, adding relevance to the larger teaching field. On the other hand, however, these five white women do not speak for all preservice teachers; thus, no generalizability should be gleaned from this book.

As I elaborated in the methods chapter, the survey respondents were 25 elementary education majors at two higher education institutions in Massachusetts. I did not ask for their race or sex, but I recall that most of the participants I saw when I introduced this project to various classes were white women.

As for the subgroup participants in phase two, they shared similarities racially and geographically, but there were biographical differences among them and they differed in their reasons for participating in this project. The five preservice teachers were Mary Beth, Beatrice, Nadia, Beth, and Michelle. Mary Beth was just finishing her freshman year. She is from a working/middle-class household in Connecticut. She described herself as a "movie person," and said because of that she found the topic of my study interesting. Beatrice was a graduating senior from a small town in rural Maine. Both of her parents are elementary schoolteachers. She was the first to volunteer and she said she volunteered because she thought the topic sounded interesting and she wanted to learn more about it. Nadia was a graduating senior. She is from a working/middle-class suburb of Portland, Maine. Her mother teaches English as a second language to adults, and Nadia often spoke about her international friends as a result, which gave her a sense of worldliness that the others did not possess. She described herself as curious, and she discussed how she enjoys "tearing things apart," including the media, which is why she said she volunteered. Beth, originally from Long Island, was a graduating senior from a large urban northeastern school, a school that has an excellent reputation for its teacher education program. She was the only participant from this school in phase two. During her teacher education program she focused on math and computer science, which she stated was why she was interested in participating in this study, in order to expand her knowledge base in various types of media. Michelle was at the end of her freshman year. She is the only child of a very successful businessman (her father owns a chain of retail stores in New England), and she grew up in Rhode Island. When she initially volunteered by e-mail she told me she might not stay within the elementary education major; that she might switch to psychology (child psychology in particular). Psychology is what she claimed piqued her interest in this topic. Following is a deeper introduction to each of these five subgroup participants.

Mary Beth

> I've gone to the movies about every week. I'm a very movie person. I love the big screen. Um, TV, I watch a couple hours a day. I try not to here at college, but it's hard. Um, I'm very good with the Internet and computers, word processing and all that, and then the Internet, looking up stuff, knowing where to go. And, like, I don't know, I just, I learned all that at a young age, and I've just grown from it. And I go with technology, like the newest things usually; I'm there with it. (Interview, 5/2/01)

Mary Beth's media interests correspond with her desire for intrapersonal awareness and growth. For Mary Beth, the media portrays reality, and therefore she believes that media texts can teach in positive ways, particularly when it comes to identity formation.

> Um, for me they teach me a lesson. Like *Boston Public,* it is their first season, but it's all about teaching. Even though it's high school level, it's just about teaching. And they do the real issues that are arising in today's [schools], in the year 2001, about gun control, drugs, hit lists, like all that. Every issue is usually something that's already happened in one of our schools. And they just put it on television. Then like WB [Warner Brothers network] shows, most of them are like *Buffy* [*the Vampire Slayer*], of course that's not real, you know vampires, but like, just like how she deals with life and being a slayer and stuff. I take, see like that's, movies I'm the same way. I take stuff out of movies and relate it to my personal life, and that's why I *love* going to the movies, and I love like watching TV, certain shows, and because I take stuff out. Like, my mom doesn't think this. She kind of "you spend too much money going to the movies," but I do it because I get stuff out of my life that's forming who I am. I'm finding out more stuff about me when I watch movies that deal with stuff that has issues. . . . (Interview, 5/2/01)

During a discussion of the movie, *She's All That,* Mary Beth confided in me by sharing deep intrapersonal struggles she has had in her life, like low self-esteem, and she explained how various media texts, like *She's all that,* for example, have helped her problem-solve these issues.

She spoke with me of television in specific ways. She referred to non-cable networks and their shows easily by name. And she also explained that she organizes her viewing by shows, as opposed to random viewing. She explained that this is different from earlier in her life when she would watch television all the time without regard to what shows were on. She explained that now she, herself, sees that there are "better" things to do in life besides "sit in front of a TV and get involved." While her parents told her she watched too much television, she has always felt independent in her viewing habits.

Interestingly, Mary Beth's growth throughout this data collection process manifested itself in terms of her expressing repeatedly that she was interested in learning more about media production (i.e., the editing process). She felt as though her vast experiences in media exposure left her begging for a deeper understanding of the processes behind the scenes in terms of the production process itself. She did not, however, express much interest in learning about the socio-cultural aspects of the media such as marketing, representation, etc.

Beatrice

Beatrice's childhood included viewing what seems like an average amount of television. That is, her parents placed very few restrictions on her, and she named for me various favorite programs, some of which they even watched as a family (Disney programs, for example). While she did not go to the movies very much because of their rural location (a two hour trip), she did play video games a lot. When she described the music she listened to (her parents' music), she illustrated for me the picture of a "happy" family taking vacations and singing to the oldies in the car. She did not have much exposure to computers growing up either at home or at school (and she doesn't seem to like them very much now). She also told me how she, her sister, and neighbors used to make home videos with made-up stories. She has few memories of media in school, but she did recall watching *Sesame Street* in kindergarten. In terms of production, she made one video in high school for a class, but it was simply a point-and-shoot video.

She seemed to feel that she currently watches a lot of TV, but she also expressed her frustration over this:

> I hate TV. I hate it, because I don't have time. I don't have time now. All
> year long when I'm in college, I don't have time to sit in front of the tel-
> evision, but when I go home for Christmas or something like that, then
> I find myself caught in watching television, and it feels really good some-
> times, but then it really annoys me a lot. Television takes up so much
> time. But I also, I use the Internet only when I have to. I really, I don't

know, I see so many people that are on it all the time that I e-mail and stuff like that. But I'm not, I don't IM. I hate IM, instant messenger.

She discussed with me her unhappiness with some aspects of the media, specifically singers like Britney Spears who attract children, but whose image she finds inappropriate:

> I have a lot of little girls come up to me and say, "Oh, I love Britney Spears." I don't know what they say, but they talk about Britney Spears, and I kind of just think in my mind. I don't think I usually say anything. I just think in my mind, "Oh, that's just too bad." (Interview, 6/14/01)

Further, she was never one to watch MTV very often. And at this point in her life, she finds parts of it annoying, particularly during their spring break productions, which she feels simply reproduces negative stereotypes about college students and a misrepresentation of college life in general.

She was unique however, in that at the time of my data collection she was enrolled in and finishing a communications course called "Children and Television." This course not only gave her familiarity with current children's programming but it also seemed to have taught her skills at considering the wider implications of children's television, such as the marketing of toys. But she claimed that if anything, it inspired her to talk with parents about how they should watch television with their kids.

Nadia

Nadia did not describe herself as a heavy television user, and her parents never restricted her viewing. She said that she has always preferred being active to being inside watching television. She did discuss participating in television viewing as a social activity, previously with her family, and now with her girlfriends when they watch an episode of *Dawson's Creek*, for example. She told me that she enjoys predicting and questioning the show's production and content, whereas her friends are more interested in discussing the content as it relates to personal relationships, etc. While she stated that she thoroughly enjoys listening to music (mostly popular/top 40 music), she said that she never really "got into" MTV. In terms of media skills, she seemed to understand that there are many techniques involved in media production, but she admitted that her knowledge is limited. What she knows technically came from a photography course in high school, operating a video camera on various occasions, and having built a Website for a college course. She said she uses the Internet frequently for research, and she judges a Website's validity by its address and/or source.

Nadia was different from the others in that she frequently stated that issues surrounding the media deeply interest her:

> I'm very interested in it because that was almost my major instead of education. I looked into communication or business advertisement. I love it and it's an interesting field, but it also has many dark sides to it, that I think is good for children to know too, many subliminal messages and things, because that's what advertising, a lot of it is. (Interview, 5/2/01)

Nadia discussed her beliefs of what she called bad media with sparing examples, yet she also felt strongly that it is important to acknowledge the good of media as well. For example, during one of our discussion groups, she said,

> I think if it's used in an appropriate way, it could be very beneficial to us. I think sometimes, out in media, they use it to sell, to make money. They use it in ways that a lot of people perceive as negative, because it's influencing violence. I mean there's different sides and different takes on it. But I think it could be used really positively if you take, like a movie, and you take the camera point of view and the angles and the lighting, or photography and you look into that, or radio, the benefits of radio and you teach that to kids. But right now, I feel like there is a lot of negative in media. There's a lot of gender issues; there's a lot of racial issues. There's a lot of negative things out there. And that seems to be what people are focusing on more than anything. I know even in my college courses I learn about the negative stuff about media. Where I haven't learned that much about the positive aspects, and I'm sure there are plenty, because it's out there, and it's surrounded us for this long. There's got to be something good about it. It helps our economy; you know, there's got to be some positive thing to it, otherwise, why has it gone on so long; wouldn't we have stopped it[?] It gets out the products, and lets the consumer know what's out there. I think kids need to know the positive things of it too, and not just the negative. (Focus Group 1, 5/9/01)

She elaborated on the negative effects of media with a personal example of her eight-year-old cousin who is concerned about her weight because of the images she sees on TV and in magazines. Mostly, however, during the conversations, Nadia expressed herself as above, as a seeker who also acknowledged the importance of including media texts in classrooms.

Beth

Growing up in a middle-class suburb on Long Island, Beth said she did not watch a lot of television. She said her college-educated parents placed restrictions on her, because they preferred that she engage in other activities such as reading or sports, and they considered some programming "bad" (e.g., *Beverly Hills 90210*). While Beth described her media consumption as less than her peers, she said she never seemed to feel as though she were missing anything.

Currently, she said that she uses the Internet frequently, for e-mail, newspaper headlines, and generally as a telephone book/resource guide. She said she watches a "little" television now as a social activity; specifically, she got hooked on the reality show *Survivor*. She also said she likes to watch movies either at the theater or on cable television, and her preferences seemed to lean toward comedies. As for MTV, she said she watches it for its shows, like *The Real World*, or its various game shows, but she did not express any interest in music videos. Again, she separated herself from her peers by saying that they can watch music videos for hours, whereas she could care less, even if the music appeals to her.

She was aware of the existence of varying production techniques, but not to a deep level. For example, she felt that the producers of the show *Survivor* used techniques from the reality show, *The Real World*, to create cliff-hangers. She was made more aware of production techniques from an experience she told me about from the previous summer when she went to see the taping of an MTV show's episode in Boston:

> They were taping one of the [segments for *Road Rules/Real World Challenge*] in downtown in Boston, and it was a, I don't know if anybody watches that show, but it was just aired a couple weeks ago. They were doing a mud wrestling contest, like the Road Rules team goes against the Real World team, and they have to like mud wrestle each other in this competition. And what I was telling Stephanie was that we waited in line to get into this place for like 3 hours, and the people were all running late, so we waited in line, waited in line. We finally got in, and we were inside, like they were doing the competition back and forth for like 2 and 3 hours and then when it was over they all jumped on each other, and they were all like really fun, and they were talking to us and all that kind of stuff. And then, when it aired a few weeks ago, it's like a 22-minute show, and that's it. It was like half the show was inside when they were doing the mud wrestling, and that was it. And it was cut and pasted and kind of put together so that you would only see certain parts of it. And even, people that my friends and I remembered seeing like wrestling each other, oh but they didn't show that. And they made it look like they were wrestling, not that they were wrestling different people, but they made it look a lot different than it actually was. When we were like sitting in the front row, and we were like, "we're going to be on TV, and this is going to be so great." And we could like see ourselves flash by for like a second and that was it. And they really cut it down a lot. (Discussion Group 1, 5/9/01)

When we talked about media that she dislikes, and the topic of musicians came up, she spoke somewhat contradictorily. That is, she said she believes in freedom of expression for the musicians, yet she expressed a paternalistic feeling toward kids' exposure to some lyrics. She felt as though children do not understand what they listen to, and therefore, sometimes children look up to some of the musicians whose messages she feels are negative, like the rap artist Eminem for example.

Michelle

During her childhood, Michelle's parents restricted her media consumption a lot, but she claimed it never concerned her. Now she said she understands why they did this; "it's a waste of time," she believes. She also said that her parents called television "stupid." She didn't have posters of celebrities on her walls; she didn't have any particular favorite bands or singers; she did not name any movies that she has liked a lot; yet at the same time, she never felt disconnected to any of her friends:

> Obviously, I think, like, out of most kids, I didn't watch that much television; I wasn't exposed to that much media. I mean my parents like tried to get me to read books and look at the newspapers, and stuff like, but I didn't really want to do that. But as far as TV, I didn't watch that much of it.

Twice Michelle mentioned her belief that television is addictive, particularly soap operas, daytime and nighttime. She explained that because she felt they were addictive at an early age, she practiced self-control so she would not get hooked.

She wrestled uncomfortably with the idea of the media's influence, particularly when it comes to violence. At first she mentioned that she did not believe it has the power to influence us, yet things such as cigarettes or alcohol she felt can affect children. And later, she verbally thought through the violence issues and it seemed that she decided that if she believed that cigarettes and alcohol could affect children, so could media violence. Still later I found out that she wrote a paper on this in a college course in which she argued that media violence had no (or little) effect on us, but through her verbalization with me, I think she realized that she felt differently, which left her feeling somewhat uncomfortable.

In terms of believability and/or bias, she claimed that she does not really consider or question things in general, but a college course she took in sociology in which they discussed issues in deceptive advertising got her thinking differently. She said that before the course she tended to trust things in the media, and that she never gave those issues a second thought. And so it was her college course that first gave her reason to stop and consider the deeper aspects of the media.

As with another participant, she felt that an advantage of teaching kids about media literacy corresponded with a child's curiosity and ability to learn things at a young age. In other words, much like Mary Beth spoke of children learning languages efficiently at young ages, so too did Michelle speak of the advantages of children learning concepts such as media literacy, which she saw as kids understanding that not everything is real. This was a predominant theme on which she continued to express herself—that so much of the media is "not real," and that is what she felt we all need to understand.

Toward the end of her first interview, Michelle seemed to get frustrated because she discovered that she believed that print is good and visuals are bad, but she seemed to know that this should not be true. For the last page of this transcript she expressed frustration over not exactly understanding what this idea of media literacy is all about—that is, is it celebrating media? Is it asking kids to "read" something that they may or may not be interested in? Is it telling kids what's good and what's bad? (She mentioned that this seems to get into moral issues.) And she concluded uncomfortably with the statement, "I guess there really is no right or wrong."

OUR DISCUSSIONS

For the first discussion group I wanted to delve deeper into particular topics from the survey and their interviews, topics about which I wished to know more as well as things that surprised me. This was their first time meeting as a group, and only two of the subgroup participants knew each other. Perhaps because of this, the discussion flowed in an orderly manner at the beginning without the participants commenting on each other's ideas frequently. By the end of this first session, however, the atmosphere was more conversational with laughter breaking out.

I began by asking the group if they had had any additional thoughts about the media or media literacy since the interviews. It was at this point that they each expressed their desire to know more about the topic in general. Specifically, Beth related a story from her current teaching experience in which she thought about how much unsupervised television viewing her urban students must have in relation to her own suburban upbringing. This led to a discussion of parental involvement/presence in relation to children's media consumption (I delve into this issue in the next chapter).

After this general introduction, the questions I asked seemed to be of a random nature because there were various topics in which I wished to know more about in relation to media and media literacy. First, we began to discuss about media literacy, or teaching media production to students, through my asking for their ideas on how to teach kids to tell a story with images or video. They provided various ideas going from asking kids to tell a story based on a picture(s) and vice versa. Beth even described an activity in which students might take an existing story and create storyboards, which are like illustrated cartoon blocks that relate stories in sequence.

Next, I asked them what they know about advertising, demographics and marketing. After this we discussed how influential they felt the media are in relation to our culture, and then whether they felt that the media did more good things or bad things for society. This was a full discussion that leaned more toward how the media affect all of us more negatively. That led to their expressing thoughts on when children should question things in the media. Here most of the participants felt that it would be good for children to learn to question things as they go along in their schooling. But Beth felt otherwise, as she thought it would not be healthy for young children to question everything they see. I also asked them about identity formation and media influence in terms of when it begins and how long it lasts. They indicated that media affect us from "womb to tomb." Next, we talked about their general dislike for documentaries, which led to my questioning their awareness of "alternative media" (I did not define this for them; instead, I was trying to gauge their degree of media access; i.e., do they consult independent press sources? Do they watch independent or "art house" films? etc.). Their lack of awareness of what I meant by alternative media practically became an on-going joke until I revealed what I meant in our last session. After this I wondered if they felt that media literacy needed to be identified for what it is. In other words, does media literacy always need to be called "media literacy?" I explained that I was curious about this as a result of their having given me examples of media literacy experiences from classes (mostly college, non-education courses), yet they seemed unfamiliar with the term and its components. They generally felt that knowing the term and its components better would be helpful. Next I asked Beth to describe the professional media production experience she had shared with me during our interview, and I asked others if they had similar experiences; no one else had. As a final question I wondered what more they wished to know about the topic of media literacy. Here Mary Beth and Nadia expressed interest in learning more about media production, editing, camera angles, etc.

After this general question and answer session, the group watched two short videos, one a music video of Madonna's, and the other a Canadian public service announcement about critical television viewing. I asked them individually what they thought of each one, and afterward, we returned to our room and had a general discussion. They discussed Madonna's video first, and their expressions ranged from an analysis of the values it presents, to how different viewers might "read" it differently, to how it is rather disturbing, especially in relation to the song itself, which a couple of them had heard on the radio prior to viewing the video. I elaborate on their ideas in later chapters. By the time they discussed the "House Hippos" video, they were giggling and not talking in such an orderly fashion as earlier. They generally expressed surprise over the direction of this video's content, as they at first thought it was going to be a commercial for some particular product. This led to a discussion on how the content of commercials can sometimes feel totally unrelated to the products. They were also surprised that such a video exists because they did not seem to think that any media producers would want viewers to question what they watch.

The second discussion group, as I described in the previous chapter, consisted of two case-method problems (McNergney, 1994). In chapter six, I elaborate on each of these as it relates to media literacy pedagogically. More generally, this group session felt more relaxed with the participants laughing more often and contributing in more of a conversational manner. I began with a similar question as from the beginning of the first session regarding their thoughts about media and media literacy since the last group meeting. Beth mentioned that she had thought about Madonna's music video some more and particularly how when she heard it on her car radio she thought differently about the song. Beatrice raised her curiosity over the formal definition of media literacy, and Nadia said that she had been feeling a heightened sense of awareness about various types of media, including a deeper acknowledgment of their being ever present.

After this initial question we began Case A, which lasted 15 minutes. I acted as a facilitator during their discussion by asking them questions that attempted to place them in this precise scenario. For example, in one instance when Beth suggested that the child should justify his reason for bringing in the video, I asked if there was another route to take to be respectful to this student.

For Case B, they began by perusing through class sets of 6th graders' media preferences for 10 minutes, during which time they were definitely conversational. There was much laughter, many eyebrows were raised, and quite few times I heard, "oh my word." They not only expressed sadness and fear over the children's media preferences, they also often expressed how surprised they were that the parents were allowing their children to watch certain movies and TV shows. Eventually they discussed how sad they felt over the students' loss of innocence. Though I did not give them any time constraints, for the next 40 minutes they worked together to build two lessons related to the 6th graders' media preferences using a template I provided (I explain this in detail in chapter six). They divided themselves up into various roles (a recorder for the brainstorm, Beatrice; a recorder for the final copy, Nadia; and Mary Beth provided the explanations from a sheet I gave them explaining the various areas required in the lesson plan template). The three seniors did most of the talking during the lesson planning, and at no time did they appear to become wildly distracted or tired. In fact, they continued to express themselves thoughtfully for the final question on what more they wished to know about media literacy. This led to their expressions of excitement over these types of lessons in schools as they felt that lessons such as these would greatly pique the interest of children.

In the previous chapter, I provided a description of this third discussion group, which was centered on the viewing of the video *Signal to Noise*. What is important to add here, however, is that for this discussion group, the participants showed their increased comfort level by talking and making eye contact with each other much more instead of looking at me when they made comments and/or answered questions. Perhaps this was due in part to the fact that they had made notes on the work sheet I provided them (see appendix) before watching the video.

For the fourth discussion group, beyond what I already described in the last chapter, I must add here that, again, I began with the question about what they had thought of in relation to media literacy since our last meeting. This time four of the participants were in the middle of their final exams and two remarked on media-related issues in their exams. Beatrice described a final exam question she was writing for the Children's Television course related to an analysis of "alternative media" toys, which still stumped the group. Mary Beth talked about how within a science course she had to include a media critique related to science—she critiqued an article from a science magazine. Nadia discussed how she had recently talked about media literacy with her cooperating teacher. The teacher asked Nadia what she had found out about it from this research project, and Nadia was surprised that she knew more about this subject than the teacher. Once again, this final group session had a strong sense of cohesion, which was apparent in their conversational style and eye contact. Clearly they had established mutual respect and trust as the four sessions progressed.

In terms of the media literacy website they examined, what was most surprising was the degree to which only one of the participants, Mary Beth, listed multiple items she had explored in the site. The others mentioned one or two items they found interesting, but Mary Beth, on the other hand, expressed the deepest examination as related to the site and its links on media literacy. Finally, after they brainstormed together a list of standards on media literacy both for students and teachers (see Table 2 below), what was interesting was their link at that point to other disciplines. It was in their deepening recognition of media literacy's components that enabled Beth to see connections with technology, and Nadia and Beatrice connected them to reading/print literacy.

This chapter has provided a foundation for understanding the analysis that is in the forthcoming chapters. In the next chapter I focus exclusively on the media as a subject matter, the participants' personal histories with various media and their interpretations of the media for themselves, children and our society at large. And in chapter six I delve into their thoughts and analyze them in terms of teaching this subject matter.

Table 2.

Media Literacy Standards for Students

- Children should be able to understand the role that media play in our everyday life.
- Children should know different types of media.
- Children should be able to recognize biases that are present in media.
- Children should effectively create different kinds of media.
- Children should distinguish between real and fantasy media. (What is the purpose of the particular media?)
- Children should recognize strategies used by media (lighting, pitch, etc.).

Media Literacy Standards for Teachers

- Same as above.
- Teachers should be able to understand and analyze media.
- Teachers should be able to understand consequences of media (culture, race); Teachers need to instruct without biases.
- Teachers should be educated on using different types of media technology and on intertwining it into the curriculum.
- Teachers should be able to instruct it, the limits, etc.; need to know how to break it down.
- Teachers need a higher level of media literacy.
- Teachers need to be able to convince students that media literacy is important.
- Teachers should be able to apply appropriate media in an integrative fashion in all content areas.

Chapter Five
Preservice Teachers and Media/Popular Culture

In this chapter I provide an orientation and analysis of how the preservice teachers in my study talked about their media "worlds" and media in the world, or their "subject matter content knowledge" (Shulman, 1986, p. 9). This includes rich descriptions they provided me with in the on-line survey, interviews and discussion groups. The major purpose of this chapter is to create a portrait of how a group of undergraduates in elementary education conceptualize the media and popular culture. This corresponds with Shulman's pursuit of understanding preservice teachers' "intellectual bio-graph[ies]—that set of understandings, conceptions, and orientations that constitutes the source of their comprehension of the subjects they teach" (p. 8). Also, like Shulman, the assessment of these preservice teachers' media literacy content knowledge did not result simply from an analysis of the objective survey questions but also from rich dialogue from interviews and discussion groups where they viewed and commented on media material. The knowledge and experiences they shared then began to offer a glimpse at the extent to which they understood the media and popular culture.

This chapter begins with a general sketch of how these preservice teachers said they experienced media and popular culture in their pasts as well as in the present. This includes their preferences and exposure to media at home. Following that section I consider how they recalled these experiences at school. Moving beyond exposure, in the third section I provide a glimpse at how they analyzed and generally talked about popular culture for themselves. Fourth, within our discussions, the influence of media in and on our culture to sway our actions and beliefs was an important concept, and therefore merited its own section. Finally, their beliefs on the relationship of media with children are featured.

THEIR MEDIA CONSUMPTION

It is important to begin the data analysis by laying down a historical/biographical sketch of these preservice teachers in relation to media and popular culture. Thus, in this section I illustrate and analyze how they consumed media as children. For teacher educators, knowing how they say they were exposed to popular culture as children is as important as knowing how much future teachers may have spent time reading at home as children (Rummel & Quintero, 1997). In other words, if I were studying print literacy, it would be important to know if they were read to as children, and/or the extent to which their families valued reading. Knowing this information could help a teacher educator shape a literacy course that results in undergraduate students feeling challenged, satisfied and excited to go into a classroom and share a love for reading with their students. A rich understanding of the participants' preconceptions surrounding media will help teacher educators either to design a course on media literacy or to understand better how to integrate it within existing teacher education curriculum in a way that would enhance what students already know and value. In addition to having information about their past interactions, it would naturally also be important to have this information for the present as well, which I also provide in this section.

I am also beginning with a general overview of their media consumption because their experiences and opinions of a subject will undoubtedly influence their teaching and student learning (Rummel & Quintero, 1997). For some time now there has been a divide between "low" and "high" culture, which has resulted in an elite bias against popular culture by those with education (and one can also extend that to white and upper middle class)(Considine, 1997; Giroux, 2000). The tragedy that can potentially result from this within an elementary classroom is one in which the students feel denigrated by a teacher who does not value their home culture (which might include higher levels of media consumption and an appreciation for popular culture). The extension of this argument of course leads to the child shutting down in terms of his or her learning overall, because he or she does not feel valued. Instead, teachers need to value and/or care about their students' interests, for it is in this way that students' intrinsic motivations for all learning can be activated (Noddings, 1984; Sanacore, 1997). Preservice teachers then would benefit greatly from leaving their teacher education programs with a solid foundation in media analysis and evaluation and sensitivity to their future students' "media worlds."

The various media my participants responded to within the survey included television, magazines, radio, newspapers, movies, video games, and the Internet. According to the on-line survey, as children a little over half of the group (52%) watched an average amount of television (which I described in the survey as 3 hours per day) growing up, while the others watched less than average. Only two participants claimed that they watched more. A majority said they used to read one to two magazines per month (80%), listen to one to two hours of radio each day (56%), read the newspaper one or more times weekly (64%), watch one movie a month (56%) and surf the Internet on rare occasions (24% said they were online less than one hour a day). A minority played video games (44%), and then less than one hour a day. (See Appendix A for survey questions and results.)

It is important to acknowledge here that these figures and the information below are self-reported perceptions, which may neglect awareness for the ubiquity of media. That is, while these participants seem to be portrayed as less than average in terms of media consumption, this data do not consider the many incidental experiences we all have with media. For example, as we travel along our nation's roads and highways we are subjected to multiple versions of product advertising on billboards and the like. Or when we are in waiting rooms there are either complementary magazines or a television could be present. And so again, while they may report that their media consumption is somewhat low, perhaps they did not consider the ubiquity of media in our lives. Nevertheless, these self-reports reflect these preservice teachers' values at this time in their lives.

When we are young, parents can affect our media consumption. Eighteen (72%) of the survey respondents claimed that their parents were "somewhat restrictive," a term that I did not define precisely for them but instead allowed them to compare with the other responses of "very restrictive," or "not restrictive at all." This is interesting in relation to a recently published study (2000) that showed restrictive television guidance for 10- to 11-year-olds led to "a reduction of media consumption" (Van den Bulck & Van den Bergh). I conclude from this alone that this group's active media participation as children was less than average. In fact, Beth's statement here was similar to that of most of the others:

> [G]rowing up, television wasn't a big thing for me, and I've never, I didn't really pay attention to the news, because we didn't watch TV, and we never really were around. I was outside a lot, and playing sports, and I'd come home and do my homework and read a book. That was pretty much it. When I was in junior high and high school, I would read

magazines, like *Teen Magazine* or *YM* or that kind of stuff, but even in high school I didn't really watch TV. (Interview, 5/3/01)

Not only in Beth's situation was a substitute for television viewing mentioned but other participants also stated that they preferred playing outside to participating in media consumption.

When members of the subgroup fondly discussed their media preferences as children, it was usually popular music that garnered the most endearing expressions. Three of the respondents told me with a giggle that their first concert was New Kids on the Block.

> New Kids On The Block was the original "boy band" of [19]90's. They sold records by the millions with their [rhythm and blues]-inflected bubblegum pop, filled concert halls with screaming girls wherever they went, and dominated teen magazines with their hunky, yet clean-cut image (Yesterdayland, 2000, para. 1).

It is important to acknowledge that this band was created by a music producer and then packaged to appeal to preteen girls. While these participants shared their fondness from this time in their childhood, they did not pause to reflect on and share why it was that they were fans (i.e., a targeted market group). They also mentioned various television shows and Disney movies that were childhood favorites, but nothing resounded collectively as their shared enjoyment for popular music. Mary Beth was the one participant who described an abundance of television shows and movies that were her favorites.

As for their current stated media consumption, a large majority of the survey respondents said they watched less than three hours of television per day (68%), read one to two magazines per month (76%) and about one newspaper per week (56%). A large number stated that they never play video games (88%) and that they are on the Internet less than three hours each day (64%). A little less than half claimed that they listen to the radio more than three hours each day (40%) and go to the movies about once a month (48%). There is obviously much more Internet usage now, but even there it seems to be mostly relegated to research and basic e-mail, according to the subgroup. Beyond my general questions regarding the Internet, they mentioned that "instant messaging" (IMing; online synchronous communication) was somewhat popular among their peers in the dorms, but their own usage seemed rather minimal. It appears then that their media consumption currently is even less than their consumption was while growing up, Mary Beth included.

Again, the media texts they now prefer are varied, but all are within the "mainstream." For example, the media texts they discussed and shared were, for television, from the major networks, cable and non-cable; for movies, they discussed the big budget Hollywood movies; and for newspapers, they described reading their local newspapers. When asked if they ever access "alternative media," no one in phase two knew what that meant. I purposefully did not define what I meant by alternative media until our last discussion group meeting, because I assumed that if they accessed alternative media, they would know what it meant. By alternative media I meant media that are generally not distributed by foremost producers, such as the major networks and publishers.

While she clearly stated that she participates in large amounts of media consumption, within the subgroup and among the survey data results Mary Beth could be considered the outlier. The theme that emerges from a look at these preservice teachers' media consumption, both past and present is that they claim to participate in media and popular culture to a minimal extent; they do not feel that the media play a big role in their lives. However, as I stated earlier, there could perhaps be a difference between what it is that they claim to experience in terms of media and what they are exposed to de facto.

MEDIA EXPOSURE IN SCHOOL

While the above section elaborated on the media background of the participants as children at home, it seemed that it was also important to get a sense of how they may or may not have been exposed to media and popular culture during their schooling. According to Pamela Grossman (1990) "many of teachers' ideas of how to teach particular topics can be traced back to their memories of how their own teachers approached these topics." Many other educational scholars have echoed this belief (Britzman, 1991; Feiman-Nemser, 1983; Lortie, 1975; Nespor, 1987). For this reason, it seems imperative to have a sense of how preservice teachers recalled media being used (or not) within their own classroom experiences. Hobbs (1997) noted that elementary teachers have often utilized video in the classroom for "non-educational purposes." She further illustrated examples of what she calls misuses of video in classrooms as follows:

- Students view videotape with no opportunity to discuss, ask questions, pause or review material.
- Teacher mentally disengages while the TV is on in order to get "real work" done.
- Teacher uses TV viewing to reward class.

- Teacher uses media only to get students to pay attention to the subject matter.
- Teacher uses video to keep kids quiet and under control. (p. 4–6)

A little over half of the survey respondents (56%) said that they watched videos at school (K-12) about once a month, with the remainder claiming less than that. When they did watch a video, a little less than half (48%) said both that they watched videos either as a reward or as content-related support. In terms of media production, a majority never produced any media in school (56%), which I defined in the survey as videos, radio programs, etc., nor did their teachers ever discuss the production of a video (64%). A small number (24%) used the Internet on a weekly basis, but most never used it or only used it about once a semester. When I asked members of the subgroup what they recalled their teachers doing while they watched a video, Nadia said, "Normally the teacher was sitting at the desk correcting, probably catching up, probably planning. Probably using it as crunch time to get stuff done." (Interview, 5/2/01)

During the discussions of the media and schooling, Beth recalled a third grade teacher who was categorically anti-television. Beth said the teacher told her mother that an hour of television a day was too much. When I asked her how influential this teacher was on her family, she replied:

> Oh, very . . . I know it was influential on my family, because I know that the whole time I was growing up, I'd never watch TV. I mean, I tell people now, when I was, all the way through high school I never watched TV during the week, because my third grade teacher said that TV was bad. . . . My parents kept that in their heads, so I never watched TV throughout high school. (Interview 2, 6/11/01)

Nespor's (1987) words here are resounding. A "crucial experience or some particularly influential teacher produces a richly detailed episodic memory, which later serves the student as an inspiration and a template for his or her own teacher practices" (p. 320). Given Beth's experiences and Nespor's analysis, it would follow that Beth might have a tendency in her future teaching to forward the underlying notion that television is bad.

In terms of media exposure in teacher education, most of the students in the subgroup had taken a basic computer course in their teacher education program (or plan to) that focused on restructuring classrooms with technology. Beatrice's teacher education experience was similar to the other participants in that she had very little exposure to media and/or media issues within her teacher education coursework. However, during one of the interviews she described her own attempts at integrating media into a lesson during one of her field placements by using two movie clips to illustrate the concept of cooperation. She explained, "My main purpose was so that they could actually see something, instead of me always talking about it, they could actually see a visual of it." Nadia watched her first grade cooperating teacher do a lesson on Venn diagrams that had to do with various aspects of the media. She explained that at first she was somewhat skeptical of a lesson that would blend math and popular culture, but once she saw it she was convinced of its value by seeing how interested the children were in the topic:

> I know one of the kids said, "well you know in commercials and stuff like that, [they] tell us about toys, and it can be good because it makes us know what toys are out there, but it can be bad because sometimes your mom says you can't have them, and sometimes they're expensive or mom says that they aren't a good toy and stuff like that." So, from a kid's perspective, which was interesting to see, because kids totally see it different[ly]. But it was interesting that they were that insightful, and that that much was brought up in a first grade classroom, but I also think that it's also because [the teacher] encourages it so much. And she tries to bring media in as much as she can, even though the resources are limited at this school. (Interview 5/2/01)

When I asked Beth whether she discussed issues of media influence or analysis in her teacher education coursework, she recalled a discussion about Channel One from an educational technology class in which they considered the various aspects of in-school commercialization, but she expressed no lingering opinions about the topic. In her student teaching field placements, Beth also saw basic media usage. For example, in one classroom she was in, the teacher used an instructional science video for a topic she was not comfortable teaching, and in another example Beth saw the media being used as a reward and/or babysitter just before the winter holidays. Neither Mary Beth nor Michelle had any exposure to media issues in the few teacher education courses they had taken as freshmen.

In terms of college exposure to popular culture/media in their non-education courses, a majority (64%) of the survey respondents claimed that they never studied the media in college, but among the subgroup it was more prevalent (this could be explained by their interpretation of the survey question). Not only does one of the colleges offer a communications course in children's television, but the professor also seemed to wield an influence that reached out to undergraduate students not enrolled in her courses (she was named teacher of the year this year and gave a media-related speech at the graduation, which influenced one of my participants so much that she felt compelled to share the story with me at the exit interview).

The subgroup participants described various media-related assignments from their non-teacher education courses, including science (a science-related media critique), English (argumentation for or against *Jerry Springer*, and persuasion in advertising), sociology (persuasion in advertising), and psychology (media violence and children). While Mary Beth described one of these types of assignments she had completed, she did not seem to understand its ramifications. For an English assignment she had to compare details from two advertisements, yet she did not understand what she gained from this overall, even though it obviously required her to look deeply at advertising techniques and aesthetics. She said, "I probably did gain something. I can't touch on it right now. I like . . . I probably . . . I gained a little bit of advertising, what advertising is." In Michelle's profile in chapter four I described her discussion on media violence and children, and as I described it seemed as though she was still struggling to make connections as we spoke. Perhaps there is difficulty in transferring non-education-related content matter to the education field.

My findings suggest that this group of preservice teachers has experienced media usage in the classroom, both K through 12 and college, rather minimally, with rare opportunities for media analysis and production. On the occasions when media usage was present, it was generally congruent with Hobbs' (1997) description of media for non-educational purposes. Additionally, perhaps there are ways to think about how content learned in non-education courses can somehow be transferred for pedagogical consideration. The larger ramifications here suggest that these preservice teachers' school media histories may be a template for their future teaching, thus minimizing chances for integrating media, and ultimately media literacy, unless intervening instruction and opportunities to interact with media in the context of teaching and learning are somehow included in their teacher education.

THEIR ANALYSIS OF MEDIA

It is important to go beyond habits and media exposure experience to gain a sense of just how preservice teachers might analyze the media for themselves. This is somewhat problematic given the aims of the study overall and the limits of this research design. An entire study could be (and should be) conducted solely on how this group analyzes media to uncover the nuances. While the design I chose to pursue aimed at evaluating their analytical abilities (indeed, below I elaborate on my conclusions with confidence), it is inhibited by limitations. The media content we viewed and discussed was outside the participants' "normal" viewing patterns and habits; however, the participants were different enough from each other to make what is "normal" viewing for one unusual for another. Therefore, while there are some limitations given the design, I feel that this section provides sufficient and rich data on which to base further studies.

This section expands on how it is that these preservice teachers analyze media for themselves, because they will need certain level of sophistication in media analysis to integrate it within their teaching. This is in line with Shulman's elaboration of content knowledge requirements for teachers. He writes that teachers "must . . . be able to explain why a particular proposition is deemed warranted, why it is worth knowing, and how it relates to other propositions, both within the discipline and without, both in theory and in practice" (p. 9). In terms of my phase two participants, I found that, like their viewing habits and media backgrounds, they varied in their analytical level of sophistication. For example, after viewing Madonna's music video, Nadia spontaneously provided a rather sophisticated analysis of the video as a constructed message about women's struggles through history. Mary Beth provided a complex understanding of the underlying values in the cartoon *Dexter's Lab*. However, at other times, it seemed as though they needed my prompts to understand the various complicated nuances in media texts and/or they simply did not discuss certain crucial media analysis issues such as media ownership, media economics, and perspective/point-of-view. Specifically, I found that they focused heavily on judging media as good or bad and they had various ways of doing this. They also discussed how they criticized the media versus viewing it critically. Additionally, for them, believability was based on repetition and reputation. And, finally, the more complex analysis occurred when, as I explained above, some of the participants elaborated on underlying values within media texts. Overall, Nadia expressed herself in a more sophisticated way in regards to analyzing the media.

While the participants expressed good and bad opinions regarding the mass media, the bad outweighed the good. Good media, according to Mary Beth, are media that can be related to one's life, media that are "true." This means to her anything from actors on talk shows to dramatic representations dealing with "real life issues." "Bad" media to Mary Beth are media that are "outrageous," such as *Jerry Springer*, which she thinks is unreal, and therefore, bad. Beth agreed with her and added that shows like *Jerry Springer* and *Cops* are just "too much an invasion of what is going on." Michelle dismisses *Jerry Springer* as "stupid." *Jerry Springer* brought out the most negative comments by the participants individually without my prompting. For Beatrice however, Howard Stern is "bad," though she did not elaborate on why she feels this way.

According to Potter (1998), describing media in the either/or manner as these participants did demonstrates their underdeveloped skills of media analysis and critique. He writes, "the task of analysis is to break messages down into meaningful components so that we can understand what the message was composed of and how those elements fit together" (p. 73). This type of analysis, he said, requires viewers to ponder reasons for judgment and not simply make an uncomplicated judgment claim and stop there. It would follow from learning about their minimal background in media studies that the participants are limited in their knowledge of the various components of media literacy, and therefore, unable to make a complex evaluation.

When asked when it is that we are critical or skeptical of media, Beth answered, "People criticize what they watch all the time. It doesn't matter what it is. It could be the news. It could be a sitcom. It could be anything. We're always criticizing what the actors are wearing or what they're talking about or those kinds of things." (Interview, 6/11/01) This quote illustrates the general difficulties these participants had separating criticism from critical viewing. This perhaps further enhances what was apparent in the previous paragraph—that it seems as though they look at media more exclusively in black and white terms, from a standpoint of dualistic thinking, instead of recognizing the gray complexities present in the social realms surrounding the media.

Generalization is an important component of analysis. Potter writes that a generalization "refers to the ability to perceive one or a few concrete examples and use them to construct a conclusion or opinion about a general trend" (p. 78), which I also call believability. One must actively experience or analyze media in order to determine what to give credence to or generally trust. And so, how is it that these preservice teachers determine what to believe? According to Beth, "I think if I see it a lot, like if I see one story a lot, or you're watching the news, and something like Columbine or something like that is a really big story, and it's on every single channel." This makes repetition an important aspect in how they determine what to believe. A second condition that generally helps them choose what to trust is reputation. In this regard, they claimed that they are likely to have confidence in media, for example, a particular Website, if the source is "famous," if it has a connection to a major network or newspaper with which they have familiarity. And while I have joined these two, it is important to note that they do not necessarily do each thing actively. That is, one could infer that they might always seek out repetition in terms of accessing sources. However, I did not find this to be the case. I found that they might rely on either repetition or reputation simply by circumstance;

in other words, through "channel surfing" and/or general accessibility to major media outlets. And so I conclude that they form generalizations from limited and mostly uncritical media exposure.

Interestingly, there is one anomaly within this analysis and that is advertising. The participants either implied or made direct statements refuting the fact that they believe advertisements simply by being exposed to them on a regular basis. For example, Mary Beth said, "I don't believe in [advertisements], the majority, unless I already have the product and I'm satisfied with what it does, that it says it does." And so it seems that with advertising they do not "fall into the trap of making faulty generalizations" by focusing exclusively "on an isolated incident and conclude that it represents the typical" (Potter, 1998, p. 78). However, this is one area in which further research might reveal otherwise given their limited experiences in media literacy and the tremendous power of advertising (Barry, 1997).

Finally, I found they exhibited their most developed abilities in analysis when it came to discussing underlying values in certain media texts. We watched a music video of Madonna's called "What it Feels Like to Be a Girl," which had recently reached the status of "controversial," nothing new to this artist. In line with the preservice teachers' other analytical statements, I simply expected general expressions of shock, surprise, enjoyment or dislike. However, I was the one to be surprised in this instance. Nadia's explains:

> I think a lot of it [is] about feminism and the constant struggle women have of meeting up and getting accepted and how they, you know, it's like this whole drastic measure things. You know? It's one extreme to the next, and how they're constantly fighting for what they think they deserve and equal opportunity, and does anybody know what it feels like to be a woman. And it's kind of her expressing her feelings. She goes to an extreme of course, but that's kind of what videos are about, is going to an extreme, and that's her artistic expression. That's how I see it. (Discussion Group 1, 5/9/01)

Here, Nadia broke down this video message into various components. She expressed an interpretation of the video that considered how the visuals and lyrics worked in conjunction to express the fundamental underlying theme of women's struggles. Additionally, she said that a purpose of music videos is to go to "extremes," thus highlighting the overall complicated possibilities for this art form. Nadia and Beatrice also expressed their belief in the presence of underlying values in advertisements. This discussion came about after viewing *Signal to Noise* in which someone in the video discussed the idea of the presence of values in commercials. Mary Beth disagreed and the following dialogue ensued:

Mary Beth: I think it's more for them to sell the products and get money, you know, than I think, values. How do you put values in a commercial? A 30-second commercial of like Herbal Essence Shampoo; what's the value of that? What would a kid get out of that commercial, except, 'Oooh, I want to get that because it made her hair shiny.' Beatrice: The value would be to look beautiful, and that appearances matter. Nadia: I think it's like subliminal values, like you don't, it's not necessarily surface, but like. . . . I know we had talked about this in one of my classes. Like if there's a woman going around the kitchen cleaning and stuff, there's a value message in there that women are the ones that do the cleaning, and they're the ones that take care of the home environment, and that's a value. It doesn't come right out and scream it; the kid doesn't necessarily get that or even know they're getting that, but they could be, that could be a value that they put into them, and you know? The guy's the one [on] TV playing football or like drinking beer or, you know? (Focus Group 3, 5/14/01)

Finally, Mary Beth, who at times seemed to accept more and read less into sociocultural ramifications of the media, provided an analysis of the cartoon we watched, *Dexter's Lab*. Weeks later during the exit interview she said, "it's coming across to kids like evil is good or destroying my best friend's lab or you know, to get even to competition. That was about competition; those two were competing against each other to have the best show and tell, right? Best show and tell." (Interview, 6/19/01) These examples illustrate that these preservice teachers have the potential for media analytical abilities in terms of spotting underlying values, but perhaps only in a contrived setting such as this. It would be interesting to tease out the potential contradictions between their awareness of these values and their believability of these same values. Just because Nadia claims she is aware of the fact that certain values are perpetuated in commercials regarding women and traditional roles, does that mean that she is less affected by them? Answers to such a question remain rhetorical here, for this study did not pursue such justification, but instead operates on the assumption that with critical analysis comes conscious awareness.

While they varied in their analytical abilities, there are various elements that they simply neglected to discuss, which advocates in media literacy claim are important. For example, in her book, *Literacy in a Digital World* (1998), Kathleen Tyner collapses many of the commonly agreed-upon aspects of media literacy. One in which these participants seem lacking is in their abilities to distinguish between the various techniques used by different mediums. They did, however, express an interest in learning more about the aesthetics of media making, but they admitted their lack of awareness in this topic.

Another aspect that they skirted connects with the commercial aspects of the media. While they have a basic knowledge of marketing issues in relation to media (i.e., they generally understand about target marketing), they never talked about the concentration of ownership and media conglomerations and their effect on media production and distribution.

Potter has developed a typology of media literacy, defining eight stages we move in and around. He calls these stages "acquiring fundamentals, language acquisition, narrative acquisition, developing skepticism, intensive development, experiential exploring, critical appreciation, and social responsibility" (p. 14/15). The first three stages, he claims are typical developmental stages occurring in the first years of life. Next, in developing skepticism children between the ages of five and nine may begin to question claims made in advertising. While Potter says this is a fluid typology, he also states that

> [M]any people stay in the Intensive Development stage the rest of their lives, because this stage is fully functional—that is, people in this stage feel they are getting exposure to the messages they want and getting the meaning they want out of those messages. (p. 13)

The last three stages are considered more advanced, for they require new and deeper levels of specified knowledge. In experiential exploring, media consumers are in a stage of satisfying curiosities in terms of seeking out wider accessibility. Those at a critical appreciation point might look at the varied aesthetic and socio-cultural aspects surrounding a media text. Finally, for social responsibility a person might consider taking a "moral stand that certain messages are more constructive for society than others" (p. 15).

After analyzing these preservice teachers' analytical abilities it seems that they too are generally arrested in the intensive development stage. In other words, they did not express themselves as searchers for "a much wider range of messages," as those in the experiential exploring stage might. Nor were they like those in the critical appreciation stage who "see themselves as connoisseurs of the media [seeking] out messages that are better cognitively, emotionally, aesthetically, and morally." And, they did not express themselves in terms of going beyond interpretation and toward social change, as one would do within the social responsibility stage.

MEDIA AND CULTURE

Understanding how it is that preservice teachers analyze media for themselves is important, but this analysis must correspond with how this group views media in relation to society at large. Perhaps a subtitle for this section could be "their understanding of the media's power." There is much written on issues of power and the media, particularly within the field of cultural studies. This topic could easily merit its own study as well. Ron Lembo (2000) writes that "cultural studies analysts propose to interrogate directly how the power of [the media] actually meets the social experience of people who [experience] it" (p. 55). In this section, however, I am not attempting to "interrogate directly how the power of [the media] actually meets the social experience" of preservice teachers. Instead I am seeking to understand further how it is that preservice teachers feel about power and the media in general and how they believe it impacts the social experience of others, namely children. Without having had instruction in media literacy education or critical pedagogy/theory (which I did not ask directly), I assume that this may have been one of the first times that these individuals articulated their beliefs on such matters. Because their ideas are most likely still developing, below is a rather cursory look at this topic.

They communicated strong feelings toward some media as illustrated in the previous section, and within this section I refine their expressions of fear that some people base their lives on media "too much." The participants claimed that all of us are influenced by trends portrayed in the media throughout our life spans, whether from advertising or other media, and they were aware that the media use sophisticated means for understanding us as consumers, but they did not know precisely how this is done. With regards to the sophistication of the media, they also confirmed this awareness by acknowledging the potential for multiple interpretations of a media text, which I also expand upon below. These preservice teachers thought that media were powerful enough to be an effective escape from "reality," but they felt this was harmless every once in a while; on a following page, this issue unfolds. Finally in the last part of the section I include their feelings that aspects from the media reflect in children's behavior, specifically in a negative way.

With ease and on numerous occasions this group of preservice teachers discussed their awareness of the persuasive power they believe the media have over people's behavior, namely consumer behavior. They felt that it begins during the preschool years and continues throughout our lives. For example, Mary Beth described how she thought that "business people" feel the need to have a cellular telephone as a result of successful marketing in order to "look the part," and she felt this has spread to many others as well. She described coming to college and seeing how easily her classmates rationalized obtaining cell phones instead of paying what they felt were the high costs of the campus telephone services. With regard to the power of the media, Nadia said, "[I]t's almost like the media, kind of, I don't want to say programs us, but it kind of, you know, makes us who we are, and if you don't wear that certain type of shoe or that certain brand of clothes, you're not cool or you're not, you know? So it kind of forms everything we are." (Focus Group 1, 5/9/01)

While they readily expressed strong opinions on this, they became somewhat confused in trying to explain just how the media are able to do this. When I asked specifically how it is that media producers know how to influence us, Michelle said, "By surveys and like people's reactions to things, like you know if they, just as far as they're not going to have some fat person putting on an ad for clothing. They put what's desirable out there and realize that we're going to be drawn to it. I mean it's almost like false advertising." (Focus Group 1, 5/9/01) Essentially Michelle's comments at the end lend themselves to their feeling that the media are deceptive. However, when I asked the participants if they felt that media influence is more of a good thing or bad thing, Nadia simply says, "It's just the way it is." Perhaps this defeatist attitude further strengthens the notion that they feel quite powerless amidst the media, and thus are themselves "victims." In other words, their expressions show that the media are a hegemonic force.

I also found that they see the media as complicated in that they felt there can be various interpretations of a single media text. They agreed that children interpret media differently from adults, and thus have different tastes. Nadia provided a rather sophisticated analysis in terms of this idea in relation to the Madonna music video:

> I think a lot of it is up to interpretation too. Like I know, I've heard a lot of classes analyzing this song when it came out. It's like, one person could see the video totally different than another person, and I think that's where it kind of gets into scary grounds, because if a kid's watching it, one kid's going to get something from it that the other might not get, you know? Like they may not have when, when she shot the gun at the cop and water sprayed out, well a kid might miss that water part of the guy, you know of the gun? You know? So then that brings up violence issues. And it brings up all kinds of stuff, so I think a lot of it is left up to the interpreter, and that's where it gets kind of scary. If it is aired on TV, and like a third grader is seeing it and stuff. They might not get the feminist, and the struggle women have gone through, and the struggle that women still feel like they're going through for equal opportunity, because I wouldn't get that if I was in like 4th [grade] and watched that video. I would just get, "Oh there's Madonna riding around in a car being really aggressive, stealing money, shooting at people," you know? Is that what it means to be a woman? You know what I mean? I think

like the interpretation leaves so much up to the person and the level of the person. That's kind of scary. (Discussion Group 1, 5/9/01)

The fact that Nadia sees the notion of multiple interpretations in media as something "scary" supports their beliefs of the potential power the media hold over us. Additionally it supports the media literacy principle that states, "individuals negotiate meaning by interacting with messages" (Hobbs, 1997, p. 9).

The participants felt media, particularly television, was an escape for many people, including themselves at times. When I asked them what they felt it was an escape from, they answered that it was an escape from reality, schedules, and thinking in general. Beatrice said, "the purpose of watching television is not to think, just to sit and zone out." They felt that the media easily enable us to "get away," which speaks once again to their inherent perceptions of its power. Mary Beth further elaborated on the strong lure of the media:

> It's an escape from reality, from everything that surrounds everyday living for you. It just gets you out. It makes you just think of the show that you're watching that's on TV right at that time, and I do that too. That's what I do with like movies. Even though I relate them to my personal life, I'm wrapped around what I'm watching, and I have to keep watching it. And it's hard for me to separate myself to do something else if I'm really watching it, because I just get really into it. And it's an escape from what's around. It's an escape from my parents. It's an escape from my chores or my job. It's an escape from everything. I think at times everyone needs that. You know? I think at times, depending on the show that you're watching, it will be an escape from reality. (Interview, 6/19/01)

Clearly Mary Beth is enraptured by the media and seeks them out as an escape for herself, but she acknowledged this importance for others as well.

Finally, these preservice teachers often spoke about the power of the media over children, at times with grave concern. Curiously, they rarely, if ever, acknowledged their own vulnerability when they were growing up. Perhaps this is due in part because their consumer awareness abilities were not as critical as they are now. Once again, they showed their particular sensitivity to issues of gender in relation to the media. Michelle said, "[A]s far as even the commercials go. . . . If a boy is playing with little girls' jewelry and the little girl is going to be like, 'why is that boy playing with jewelry?' You know, I think that the media has a lot to do with like, the way people act and the things that they do." (Discussion Group 1, 5/9/01)

Beatrice echoed a similar sentiment during the same discussion group. "Like little girls wanting to be thin, and I say most of that comes from the media." These beliefs are notable in that they relate to the preservice teachers' understandings of child development and identity formation. They seemed to express a particular loathing for the current popular singing star, Britney Spears. In talking about her and others like her, Beatrice said, "it's the way that they dress and the way that they speak; it's not very intelligent, and the way that they portray themselves and dance, and I just don't like it for little girls to be watching, or boys, little boys, older boys." Clearly Beatrice believes that the media have a great influence on children in terms of gender, and she expressed strong feelings that the media "reflects in children's play." She described how her mother, a kindergarten teacher, told her about the influence the cartoon *Power Rangers* had on her students. She often saw her students playing using the various martial arts moves that the characters of that show performed. Beatrice was deeply alarmed by this. It would not be hyperbole to say that their general sentiments regarding the media and its power over children leaned toward outrage and disgust.

Perhaps because four of my participants had not had significant experiences in urban school settings, there was very little mention of differences in demographics in relation to media influence. Beth, however, was working in an urban school during the data collection, and at times she attempted to express a consideration for how children in poor urban neighborhoods might experience media differently from children in middle class suburban environments. But it seemed as though her ideas were still developing, as she halted her own speech to say that she had lost her train of thought.

What emerges then in terms of a theme involves our passive participation with the hegemony of the media. This idea stretches across many of the areas above in that it corresponds with their proposition that the media are quite influential in all of our lives, and we are often without the power to avoid its dominion. Second, their recognition that media can be interpreted differently by different people also speaks to its reign. And last, that the media serve as an escape from our daily realities highlights how the media are purposefully taken for granted and generally, not problematized. Another theme that emerged within this section relates to Beatrice's remarks above, which border on paternalism and are echoed in various exchanges by the other subgroup participants. This supports Masterman's (1997) thesis that most teachers have a "deep-rooted mistrust" of the mass media:

> This view of the media as corrupting influences, or virulent diseases—
> rather like diphtheria or polio—which threatened the cultural and moral

> health of us all, particularly children, is perhaps best understood as part
> of an even longer tradition of respectable middle-class fears of the cheap
> and debased amusements of working people. (Masterman, 1997, p. 20)

And so this group of participants is quite similar in their grave concern that
the media have strong control, particularly over children. In the final section, I embellish on these thoughts.

RESPONSIBILITY FOR OUR CHILDREN

Given the fact that this book is related to the education of our young, I must
admit a small level of naiveté in my initial oversight. Very few of the questions I asked my participants directly related to notions of responsibility for
our children, yet over and over they brought this issue up, further supporting Masterman. Fortunately, inductive research calls for the emergence of
themes, and therefore I could not neglect this topic they found so important.
They were outraged at the comments of a media executive in the video
Signal to Noise who expressed disregard in terms of his responsibility for
children. Beatrice said, "It makes me mad . . . that surprised me that he came
right out and said that ("We're not in the business to educate; schools are"),
and is admitting that this is how they, this is what their intent is. It's not to
educate. It's for business reasons" (Discussion Group 3, 5/14/01). But
mostly, they continuously brought up parental responsibilities when it
comes to the media:

> I think that there needs to be limits on it, and I think that parents need
> to educate their children on things like that. Even as far as like different
> bands go, like . . . as far as like, I remember, there was some big thing,
> someone was saying that their 10-year-old daughter looked up to
> Britney Spears, and she stripped on TV, you know, for the awards, and
> just things like that you know? Like kids think that that's right.
> (Michelle, Interview 1, 5/7/01)

And finally, as a segue to the next chapter, I begin to highlight their thoughts
on the field of media literacy education in schools in terms of this topic.
Below I elaborate on each idea.

While they did not express a deep awareness of media economics in
general, they were disturbed by the media executive who said "we're not in
the business to educate; schools are." Beatrice was particularly troubled
with this and was the first to comment on it after we watched the video.
After she expressed her reaction, to which the other participants quietly
agreed, Nadia asserted the complicated nature of this issue:

> I mean I don't think most media people or most don't feel like their job is to educate unless they're putting out an educational video. You know, like any program or TV show or most of them, it's not their job to take care of kids. That's the way they see it. I mean I feel like maybe they should have realized they are making an influence; they are making an impact in society, so maybe they should, but I mean, the business is in it for the money obviously. That's why they do it. That's their whole reasoning, so and that's just the way it is. (Discussion Group 3, 5/14/01)

There was a deep sense of frustration or powerlessness I felt from them over this issue, and as I heard from Nadia on other occasions during data collection, "that's just the way it is." Once again, they are implicitly expressing the hegemony of the media. And so they moved from this nebulous place where they felt that kids have little to no protection, to the one place they felt strongly in terms safekeeping our future: the home.

These preservice teachers felt resolutely that parents play a big role in a child's media consumption and level of understanding. When they discussed their personal backgrounds, they always mentioned how their parents were involved; whether they restricted their viewing, talked with them about the media, and/or generally, partook in the media with them. They so often brought up parents' responsibility that I found it interesting in terms of this particular "content" as compared to other school content in which most teachers would not necessarily "expect" such a deep level of participation by parents in their child's learning. Further, Michelle felt that it was an issue that was beyond a teacher's purview:

> It's scary and sick to think that 11-year-olds are looking up to Britney Spears. I don't know what can be done. I don't know what teachers can say or do. Or if it's like the parents that need to say something. I think the parents do play a big role, because I think they need to restrict. They're in charge of their kids. Teachers can only play so much of a role. Teachers can't tell the kids, "you can't do this; you can't do that."

Later in our discussions, she felt even more strongly that a parent's responsibility here should be great, and again she evoked Britney Spears:

> I think that there needs to be limits on it, and I think that parents need to educate their children on things like that. Even as far as like different bands go, like . . . as far as like, I remember, there was some big thing, someone was saying that their 10-year-old daughter looked up to Britney Spears, and she stripped on TV, you know, for the awards, and just things like that you know? Like kids think that that's right.

Michelle is quite stark in her opinions on this matter, and I wonder whether she might think differently if she had exposure to cultural studies. In *Understanding Popular Culture,* John Fiske (1989) wrote that "parental attempts to shield children from television's undesirable influences may actually hinder their development of the television literacy that is itself the best defense that parents could ask for" (p. 156). Once again we see that this is a complex issue in which their ideas of "protecting" our children border on unsound paternalism, which should be worked through within higher education, particularly for those who are interested in entering into an education field (Masterman, 1997).

It seemed to them that businesses are not concerned and parents are at times unavailable and/or uninvolved, which led this group to begin to see a benefit of including media literacy in our schools. By the end of our time together they acknowledged the potential of media literacy as that which can promote a child's choices and analytical abilities. Nadia perhaps expressed it best by saying:

> I think it's important for them to know what media literacy is, because they're going to be exposed to [media]; it's going to be out there. They're going to be coming, interacting with media every day, and if they're literate in it, then they can interpret it better. They can use it to benefit them, rather than, some people think that it clouds them or is negative to them, they can use it in a positive way if they understand it.

Explicating just how they understood the term and the idea of media literacy is what I will do in the next chapter.

In a synthesis study on the "Characteristics of Entering Teacher Candidates," Brookhart and Freeman found that "most . . . tend to emphasize the value of interpersonal aspects of teaching" such as "extensive nurturing and caretaking" (Brookhart & Freeman, 1992, p. 50). Given this finding, the final theme that has emerged in this chapter corresponds with this idea. In other words, the preservice teachers in my study, while corresponding with Masterman's criticism of teachers who speak about the corrupting effects of the media, are in line with what is common in most preservice teachers: the need to be caretakers. Just how it is that these two competing forces might correspond is fodder for the implications in chapter seven.

Chapter Six

Preservice Teachers' Knowledge and Teaching of Media Literacy

In the previous chapter I sought to include a rather detailed description of how a group of teacher education undergraduates has experienced and currently understands the media, or their subject matter content knowledge (Shulman, 1986). That served as a precursor to this chapter, which is an explicit portrayal of how this particular group understands and defines media literacy, and as well, how they might teach it to future students, or their curricular and pedagogical content knowledge (Shulman, 1986). Thus, this chapter moves beyond their knowledge of the subject matter content, the media and popular culture, toward their understanding of this content in a classroom setting. Knowing this is important, for it can help form curricular decisions in undergraduate teacher education. And if it is true that, as Tyner (1992) said, undergraduates in teacher education are "clamoring" for it, then teacher educators must know where their students' knowledge base begins to know where to go.

This chapter begins with a discussion of the participants' definitions of media literacy. How one defines a subject matter is related to how one understands a topic. This section not only includes various open-ended responses from the survey but also an elaboration of the five subgroup participants' definitions from the beginning of the study and the end.

It is also important to know about the participants' feelings regarding this content, particularly because in this case they express a desire to know more about media literacy education. And desire is not something to be underestimated by teacher educators. In 1989, Maxine Greene described the importance of a knowledge base for beginning teachers that allows "for the emergence of a consciousness of agency." Empowering students in teacher education to learn about content they find interesting can only work toward the benefit of their future students.

The next section discusses the participants' beliefs surrounding the preparation for media literacy, for themselves and others. I begin by elaborating on their feelings of assertiveness in handling this subject matter in the classroom. Then I discuss their thoughts on what teachers might need or want to teach media literacy effectively. During our sessions I did not ask for these needs and wants to be a part of a particular category. While I asked the question in a generic manner, much of their thoughts were similar.

Determining how they might teach media literacy was difficult to gauge given the circumstances. However, because they had not had instruction in media literacy in their teacher education to date, they had no particular plans to teach media literacy, and some of the participants were not even in a classroom, I was somewhat limited in determining how they might teach it. I found that asking them to create curricula within our discussion groups and explain how they might approach various scenarios involving students and media provided the best way to estimate their teaching abilities of media literacy. The fourth section of this chapter then includes a description and analysis of their discussions of various pedagogical issues related to media literacy education and the lesson plans they designed.

From the individuals in their classrooms, I move toward their views of media literacy in a broader sense. I felt that it was important to include their thoughts on how this field of media literacy might expand within our nation's primary, secondary, and post-secondary schools. After discussing and sharing their thoughts and experiences, they came to realize that they all lacked an adequate background in media literacy, yet they also learned that this field is mandated for schoolchildren in 48 out of the 50 states (Kubey & Baker, 1999). They found this problematic, and so this final section includes their thoughts on how its presence might expand in K through 12 settings as well as within teacher education.

DEFINING MEDIA LITERACY

When I asked the survey respondents if they knew what media literacy meant, only one person said no, while the rest were equally divided between "yes" and "not sure." Twenty-two respondents (88%) provided answers to the one open-ended question that asked for their definition of media literacy. I analyzed their open-ended responses in comparison with the most common formal definition in the United States ("Media literacy is the ability to access, analyze, evaluate, and communicate media in a variety of forms" Aufderheide, 1993). Specifically I calculated how many components of the formal definition each definition contained. In other words, if a definition contained references to "access" and evaluation" of the media, I would consider that it contained two elements of the formal definition. Some of their definitions included more than one of the formal definition's components, and only one contained all four elements. As it stood, 13 definitions contained references to access of the media, 13 to analysis, two included elements of evaluation, and five mentioned communication. Three fell outside the four terms, and two contained aspects of pedagogy. Here are a few of their responses with their categorization in parentheses:

- The ability to think critically about things you see and hear in television, radio, Internet, video games, etc. (Access and Analyze)
- Media literacy is the ability to use and understand different aspects of media (television, Internet, pictures, etc.). (Access, Analyze, and Communicate)
- Media literacy is knowing the different styles of commercials so you understand how they are trying to sell an item and why it may work best. It is understanding how to use the Internet to find information or to make information available. It is also using videos and films, and understanding the purpose behind them and how they made them. (Access, Analyze, Evaluate, and Communicate)
- Knowing how to use media equipment as well as questioning ideas presented in media. (Analyze and Communicate)
- Media literacy means being able to be literate. That is, able to understand how to use different types of media (television, Internet, computers, filming equipment, etc). (Communicate)

While these respondents provided such responses, it was still difficult to know the extent to which they understood media literacy. Perhaps these definitions reflected their intuitive abilities at defining. After all, each of the words "media" and "literacy" is a part of our vernacular. Literacy is a particularly well-known term for teachers, so perhaps they simply combined their knowledge of the individual terms to come up with such complex definitions. Additionally, perhaps they also express their limitations by simply providing the phenotypic (descriptive) response. Lev Vygotsky (1978) elaborated on the distinction between phenotypic and genotypic (explanatory) responses in such a way as to parallel my analysis of their definitions. Vygotsky described phenotypic as "the analysis that begins directly with an object's current features and manifestations" (p. 62). Their abilities to define a term by its parts may have contributed to their responses. And so, I believe these definitions lacked a more explanatory understanding of the term's depth. This became clearer after analyzing the subgroup's data (which I describe below).

I also read these definitions holistically, and one definition alone is not as strong as the combination. This idea has implied recommendations for practice that also conveniently hearken to Vygotsky. If they had taken this survey within a group environment, their collaborative efforts would have tapped into their individual "zones of proximal development," in which they would have been brought forward in their individual growth. Vygotsky defines the zone of proximal development as "the distance between the actual developmental level as determined by independent problem solving [in this case, defining the term media literacy] and the level of potential development as determined through problem solving . . . in collaboration with more capable peers" (p. 86) (i.e., defining the media literacy in a group). And so with this hypothesis, I should have expected more sophisticated, genotypic internalized responses from the discussion group participants.

During our first individual interview sessions I asked the subgroup participants to recall their definitions of media literacy from the survey. These new responses were similar to the ones above, and further, a couple of their quotes support my idea above regarding the way they "figured out" the definition of media literacy:

> [L]iteracy is kind of learning how to read, being able to read different aspects of literature, if you put media in front of that, it's kind of learning about different types of media, and being able to maybe operate different forms of media equipment. (Beatrice, 5/3/01)

> Well literacy is writing, reading and writing, and then media is videos, Internet and all that, so I just figured it was like either writing about videos, Internet and that or learning about all the media that's out there today. (Mary Beth, 5/2/01)

Given the distinctions I elaborate on above between phenotypic and genotypic understandings, examining their definitions of media literacy after they had participated in collaborative analysis and discussion activities provided a more fruitful understanding. For example, Michelle offered the following definition during our last interview, which showed her growth:

> I think it's like analyzing things, looking beyond the facts almost. I think the facts are included as in how to use a video camera, but then it's like, analyzing when you make the video. Analyzing why people might think the things they do, and what, how media plays that role, and how media's tempting to the eye, and understanding the facts about it. Instead of just saying, "well, all right, commercials tempt us." Well why? And realizing that they're spending millions of dollars to do this,

and knowing more about it. I think it's getting beyond the facts of things. (6/12/01)

In this definition she considered details of the analysis and communication aspects of media literacy. This is quite a far cry from her first answer, which was "the way media influences people." And it is also different from the survey responses with her reference to economic considerations.

Mary Beth's situation was interesting as well. At the beginning of the data collection, she held strong beliefs that her heavy exposure to media (television and movies in particular) made her more media literate than others. However, by the end she felt that media exposure was just a part of what media literacy encompasses. When we discussed this aspect at the exit interview, in fact, she said, "it's also going farther . . . learning the history of it, like how it changes over time." Her definition then expanded beyond Vygotsky's phenotypic towards a genotypic (explanatory) definition, or one that is "explained on the basis of its origin rather than its outer appearance" (p. 62).

Also interesting were Beth's two definitions in that there was very little difference from her understanding of media literacy before we began and afterwards, at least in terms of how she defined it to me. Her emphasis both times was what I came to call a "skills-based" focus. That is, some of what she (as well as others) said during our groups when we talked about media literacy in general focused on particular abilities of a media user, whether someone can program a VCR, for example, which would relate to accessing media. (I elaborate on the idea of media skills in the following section later in this chapter.) Below are her two responses:

> I guess knowing what media is; what different kinds of media are, and how to use those specifically for this project or in a classroom, or how to use media to benefit what you're teaching or to reach out to kids. (5/3/01)

> I think just knowing what different kinds of media are, how to use it, how to implement it in a classroom. I mean how to use it, like how to turn it on and program it and stuff like that, but how to implement it in the classroom. How to explain what it is and why it's important and why we're using it for this project to the class. (6/11/01)

Beyond her emphasis on skills, there is a determined focus in both of these responses on having the knowledge to integrate media in the classroom, which was similar to three of the survey responses. While this is a sound pursuit, I am also somewhat surprised that she did not articulate that media literacy involves the critical analysis of media texts, while her sub-group colleagues did. On the contrary, at one point in time, Beth questioned whether it is healthy to ask children to question everything they see and/or hear in the media, for it may lead students to become overly doubtful. In this case, perhaps this research process may have lead to her misunderstanding of media literacy as a practice that can involve not only critical analysis but also celebration of media texts.

Therefore, from this particular framing I have found that these preservice teachers were generally unaware of the components and depth of the term media literacy. And while it seems that some were partially aware of its meaning, in fact they seemed to have based their definition on its individual terms. Also emerging within this section, however, was evidence of their growth in having a deeper understanding of media literacy education after this research process. This was shown not only by their post definition growth, but as well from the standards they built for teachers and students (see Table 2 at the end of chapter 4, p. 86/87).

DESIRING TO KNOW MORE ABOUT MEDIA LITERACY

In the survey, 19 respondents (79.2%) said they wished they knew more about media literacy. Throughout phase two as well, there was a noticeable interest expressed in this topic. The initial question in the first interview in fact was why they wanted to participate in this project. Mary Beth found the survey questions interesting, and because they related to her deep appreciation for the media, she wanted to know more. Nadia felt that it would "enrich" her "current knowledge" for teaching. And Beatrice's answer sounded similar:

> [I]t just seemed like an interesting topic, since I'm going to become an elementary schoolteacher, and I, before you came in and talked to me, I wasn't really thinking I was going to integrate any media whatsoever in my classroom, because I don't know too much about it. I've taken classes, right now I'm taking a children's television class, and I'm learning about all the horrible shows for children. Also, and I took a computer course, but I don't feel as though I'm capable of teaching them certain aspects of the Internet and things like that. I just don't feel like I can teach that. So I think I'm interested in finding out, I don't know, maybe learning a few things from you I guess. (5/3/01)

In each of their responses, the word "interest" appeared; that is, they expressed interest in learning more about media literacy. Again, nearly 80% of the survey respondents expressed an interest in knowing more about it as well. It seems then that these particular participants are ripe for learning more about media literacy based on their interests alone. In fact, by the end of phase two with the subgroup participants, they were not only expressing a desire to know even more about media literacy, but they also showed an awakened awareness akin with Paulo Freire's notion of conscientization (Freire, 1989). For example, in the closing interview, Michelle said:

> I've been a lot more conscious about things, like little things on the radio and things on TV. . . . I mean, just as far as like commercials go, it's almost like a major disappointment to society, that it's like, commercials influence us so much. They're on all the time. They're on like a quarter of every TV show, like I don't know what the percentage is of time for commercials and time for TV shows. Throughout movies, they're always on right when something's getting good. Like I just think that, I feel like we're just in a fantasy world, like it's just like, you can't sit down and watch a movie on TV. It's interrupted by like, "buy this; buy that. Do this; do that." (5/12/01)

As a result of this minimal exposure to media literacy, Michelle expressed an awakened awareness of broader implications surrounding the media. Or, her interests may have acted as an intrinsic catalyst, which enabled her to be open to this new learning.

Interest and awareness however, also combined with their realization of this topic's importance for students today, which also led them toward a desire to know more about this content. In other words, they connected the topic's importance with a personal responsibility for teaching it to their future students. The following quote from Beatrice's closing interview sums up this point precisely:

> Before we started this, I really hadn't planned on doing anything with the media in my classroom, my future classroom, but now I see that it is part of life, and that it's important I talked it out I think. . . . Having me talk through it and realize that it is an important part of an education, starting very young to have media in the classroom and I think more than just having media in the classroom, to allow children to analyze it and discuss the positive and negative parts of the specific media. I've learned that. (6/14/01)

Thus, we have three motivations that have emerged from the data that support the inclusion of media literacy education for preservice teachers. First, the topic is interesting. Perhaps, this also connects with Friere's notion of "reading the world," or understanding more about those aspects of one's world that shape, define and interest us. Mary Beth falls quite neatly into this category. Second, the notion that this topic can make us move toward conscientization or an awareness of ideas/things for which we were previously unaware can be empowering. And third, these preservice teachers feel that this is an important content for kids to learn. Each of these motivations is strong, and therefore, should be nourished within their teacher education.

PREPARING FOR MEDIA LITERACY IN THE CLASSROOM

This section includes their thoughts and an analysis on the preparation for media literacy, for themselves and for teachers in general. I begin with their self-reflections in terms of their own preparation for teaching media literacy. For example, after going through this media literacy research project, the subgroup participants expressed that they still felt that they were not fully prepared to include it in their teaching. If anything, this research experience reminded them that their own education had been lacking in terms of media literacy, and they knew there was still so much that they would need to learn. Next, in terms of what they felt they and other teachers most needed to include media literacy in their classes I came to call "skills": how to operate a VCR, a camcorder, or various computer platforms; how to design Websites; how to keep up with emerging technologies, etc. In general they felt that these skills should be included in a knowledge base that needs sharpening in all teachers, for them to know more than their future students. Beyond the above mentioned "skills," however, they also acknowledged at times the need to understand how to actually teach this, and going along with that, they felt that a deeper awareness of media literacy curriculum was important:

> "But . . . really, we haven't been educated, I find, nearly enough to be going into the classroom and . . . incorporat[ing] it." (Nadia, Interview 1, 5/2/01)

This quote echoes the consensus by the subgroup regarding their self-preparedness to teach media literacy education. In the survey, when asked to complete the statement, "In helping my students become media literate, I feel . . . ," 20 respondents (83.3%) answered "somewhat prepared," while only three (12.5%) answered "prepared." It is important to digress here briefly and note that "preparedness," both in the survey and in conversation with the subgroup participants, was self-defined, with my assumption that preparedness equates with confidence.

By the end of phase two with the subgroup participants, their expressions of preparedness increased but still not to a level of fullness. For example, at the closing interview Nadia said:

I feel a lot more prepared. I feel like I'm a lot more, I feel like I've just been, it's opened a book for me. It's opened a chapter; it's opened me, gotten me really thinking about it, noticing it when I watch TV a little bit, so I feel like I'm more prepared, but I feel like there still needs to be something else. I would need more training; I would need more, like the do's and don'ts, limitations I guess of what can be taught or what should be taught at what age level; what's okay to talk about, what's not? (6/15/01)

It is important to note here also that this growth attests to the power inherent in the brief exposure that the subgroup participants had with media literacy education during this research project. Not only did their knowledge base increase but also perhaps more importantly, so did their desire.

Moving from the general ideas of preparedness to more specifics, this group expressed their opinions of preparedness in terms of skills for themselves and other teachers. By skills, I refer to the operation of media equipment and/or programs, which are related to half of the common definition of U.S. media literacy, to access and communicate media in a variety of forms (Aufderheide, 1993). The survey included various questions in relation to media skills, which might benefit a teacher. For example, 22 (86%) of the respondents said they know how to program a VCR, while 23 (92%) said they know how to operate a video camera. However, when it comes to manipulating video, only six (24%) said that they know how to use video editing equipment. In terms of using a computer for classroom media purposes, 20 (80%) claimed that they know how to create a Powerpoint presentation and 10 (40%) said they know how to build and launch a Website.

When I asked the subgroup the general question, "What is needed by teachers to teach kids about media literacy?" their answer leaned toward this notion of teachers needing skills. For example, Beth said, "They need to know how it works, like how to turn the VCR on, how to turn the television on, like very basic stuff that I've seen, a lot of teachers can't do it, and if you can't turn the TV on, how are you going to show them a movie." Beatrice felt that perhaps teachers should learn "how to operate equipment . . . and the Internet" in in-service-type courses. I see this need for skills, however, as rather limiting in terms of the overall picture of media literacy, which includes not only access and communication but also analysis and evaluation. It corresponds with Langdon Winner's ideas in relation to technology (media), in which he sees the idea of viewing technology as "technique" or "apparatus" limiting (Winner, 1977). Jason Ohler elaborates on Winner's idea in *Taming the Beast* (1999) by arguing that we must consider media beyond its skills, for "it is the big-picture consideration of technology [in this case, media] that allows us to see it in all its horror and glory, in terms of the promising but uncertain future it guarantees us (p. 25)." This could begin to occur if we think about deeper ways of including media in classrooms pedagogically.

Preparation for media literacy then also involves understanding how to teach it. In the survey, when asked if the respondents felt prepared to teach kids how to tell a story with video, 11 (44%) answered yes. However, the next question about whether they felt prepared to teach kids how to edit a video showed otherwise. Eighteen (72%) respondents answered that they were not prepared, and a majority (52%) felt unprepared to teach kids how to build a Website. Again, these are basic media "skills" that might be useful within a classroom setting so students learn how to communicate with media. In terms of teaching kids how to analyze the media, 10 (43.5%) felt unsure, while another 10 said they could not do this at all. Knowing how to teach media literacy clearly seems lacking among the survey respondents.

To reiterate Lee Shulman's (1986) ideas on pedagogical content knowledge, he wrote that it involves "the ways of representing and formulating the subject that make it comprehensible to others" (p. 9). Some of the subgroup participants seemed to understand this necessity, while acknowledging its absence in relation to media literacy education in their own experiences. For example, Nadia said, "I feel like all of what the majority of what teachers do is you know, they try to incorporate the computer once in a while or they'll pop in a video, and they count that as media literacy. I feel like a lot of teachers don't know how else. They don't have the tools. They don't know how else to incorporate media literacy. They don't know [how] to talk about the construction of a movie or the set-up." Beatrice even asked, "How are teachers supposed to keep [up] with things if they're not being taught how to teach these certain methods?"

As for their knowledge of media literacy curriculum, during our last discussion group they perused a media literacy resource Website. And not surprisingly, they expressed amazement that there was such a site and that so much media literacy curriculum existed. Nadia cited the need for curricular knowledge by explaining that in order to effectively integrate media literacy in her classroom she would need "maybe some aids, like I said, some reproducibles or some kind of lesson guidelines or something, which are available on the Internet we discovered through looking through that Website." This hearkens back to the quote introducing this section by Nadia in which she acknowledged the many questions she has in relation to media literacy education and the teaching of it.

And so it seems that while they have a certain level of preparedness in relation to media literacy, mostly in relation to some skills, they are lacking in a deeper understanding of media analysis, curricular awareness, as well as pedagogical depth. The next section highlights the pedagogical gaps even further.

TEACHING MEDIA LITERACY IN THE CLASSROOM

For this section, as I wrote above, I am basing my analysis on the discussion group case method problems that took place on May 10th:

> Submersion in a provocative case enables students to imagine things different from their own perspectives, to consider the implications of various policies or actions, and to learn of their peers' views. At the same time, they can—indeed, must—acquire knowledge and skills vital to living in a democracy. Cases can provoke students to face the many, often complex, demands of real life. (McNergney, Ducharme, & Cucharme, 1999, p. 11)

However, case methods, while effective in classroom situations, still leave much to ponder when it comes to real-time application. And so, while I can make judgments based on their dialogue, it is still somewhat limiting in determining how these scenarios might play out in a classroom. I shall describe how each case transpired among the subgroup participants and analyze each separately.

For Case A, as I described earlier, the participants were put in the role of a first grade teacher who was faced with a dilemma with media in her classroom. To reiterate briefly, she had assigned her students the task of watching a science show and bringing in three facts. Instead of bringing in facts on the day of the lesson, however, one student brought in his example on videotape and the teacher showed the video, which was a cartoon with a science setting. Our scenario ended after viewing the cartoon, and the open-ended questions began with me asking the participants what they would have done if they were that first grade teacher. The first three responses indicate their variation of thoughts:

> Beatrice: When it started to get violent, and I would have said, "okay, time to turn it off now." I just don't think that's appropriate for school.

> Nadia: I think I would have previewed it first. Like I think maybe I would have said, "Okay, you know, we'll save, if anybody has a video, we'll save it for after recess." Plan it out, you know? Or maybe have something in the morning where all the kids said what they brought. Like, you know, how many facts you brought in or something, and that way I would know that there's a video, so during a time of day I could watch it before, because just in case, because you never know what's

going to be on the tape. What if the kid grabbed the wrong tape and it was like an adult movie? I mean I wouldn't. . . . you know what I mean? But it could be anything. I wouldn't show anything on a video that a kid just brought in. I definitely wouldn't show all of that. I would edit it out.

Beth: I would be interested to see what the kid said that he learned about science from that video. I think that we could, as a teacher you can ask him before showing the video like, "Why did you bring this in? Why did you think this was a good science video?" And if he doesn't have any response, then you don't even show it. You know what I mean? If he doesn't say anything, you don't really have any grounds to just show the video, like, "okay, I'm going to take your word. . . ."

These three indicate a categorical range of responses from Beatrice not allowing the video to be shown because of its content to Nadia cautiously approaching it by previewing it first to Beth considering how she might deal with the content after the fact. And later, Michelle takes the ambivalent stance of noticing the pros and cons of allowing the video to be shown:

I can see if from both points where, I think, I don't know if I was a teacher if I would actually show that. And maybe I would talk to him after class or like before or something and ask him, like what you said, why he did bring it in. But also, just to be on his side. If I did end up showing the video in class, like I would discuss with the class, like what's real and what's not real, or like what the good things were, what they thought about it. I thought that it was a little bit violent for first graders, but just as far as like you could bring in like sharing and stuff, like as far as like when it's like show-and-tell time and you could talk about that, how it's good to share. Like I see it from both sides; I would show it and I wouldn't show it.

Perhaps the above illustrates their group-determined realization of the complicated nature of including popular culture in the classroom. Later in our discussion, they acknowledged that some of the "problem" with this scenario was in the assignment that the teacher gave to the students. One of the remedies they suggested was more explicitness in the assignment to include perhaps a list of shows from which the students could choose. Media and popular culture content and pedagogy can be rather complicated for teachers in their classrooms. Case methods only hint at the range of unforeseen issues that could arise. For example, many teachers operated "on the fly" in dealing with issues in the media after the September 11th attacks on the United States. No one predicted that such a tragedy could occur, yet it became important for teachers to wrestle with issues as they were presented by the media and think about different ways to approach the topic within their classrooms. In a November 2001 journal article, Hobbs wrote, "Months after the attack, teachers are inventing ways to integrate media literacy concepts to more deeply explore the ongoing aftermath of the September 11th attacks and the international response" (p. 407). We all hope that a tragedy of this magnitude will never again occur. However, equally shocking televised events such as September 11th, or the Kennedy assassination, or the explosion of the Space Shuttle Challenger, will most likely recur. Therefore, having the opportunity to begin to wrestle with challenging scenarios before a teacher enters the classroom could perhaps offer her much help.

Case B differed from A in that the participants were not presented with a scenario that could be altered. Instead, for Case B, the participants were provided with information (6th graders' media interests) and asked to build two lessons, as a group, which included this information for any school subject. They spent more time on the first lesson than the second as it was getting late and they were starting to drift away from the task, so they did not record details of the second lesson as they did for the first, which they wrote up on a chart (see Table 3 below) printed on a large piece of paper. It is important to emphasize here that they constructed these lessons as a group. And while I shall focus on their final products, it is also important to include some individual ideas, which were not included in the final products. For example, during their brainstorming Beth suggested the following:

> Something you could do with even the older elementary kids, like 4th or 5th or 6th graders, if you have them pick out their favorite clothing store and then ask them to make an ad for that store. Like that would give them awareness of how marketing takes place and who would they market it towards or something like that. Then that would give them an opportunity and then go out, "here's a video camera, go out and tape your commercial and bring it back and let us know why you decided to do that." Which would be interesting. . . .

Indeed, Beth's idea is interesting. First, it seems to be an implied group assignment, which has multiple known benefits (Slavin & Cooper, 1999). Second, it certainly involves the students in something that interests them (Worthy, 2000). Third, it involves various aspects of media literacy in that the students would need to have a background in marketing techniques for this assignment, thus encompassing details of media analysis. For this, they would undoubtedly learn techniques used by professionals, ideally for products with which they are familiar. This would allow them to see how they are persuaded to buy products, and it would also provide them with the analytical lenses to use when they consider how best to make their favorite clothing store attractive. The other media literacy component that the students would need to complete this project would be video production skills. Again, perhaps the teacher might do a mini lesson on camera angles, lighting, editing, and other video aesthetic techniques; more importantly, the students would have the opportunity to engage in video production or media communication.

As for other lessons that were suggested but not used, Beth also hinted at trying to design a science lesson that was related to music and sound waves. Nadia suggested a language arts lesson that dealt with point of view in relation to popular movies. And Beatrice thought that altering the setting of a popular movie might work well as a geography lesson (by researching and changing a location) or as a history lesson (by researching and changing the historical time). The group developed none of these, and their ideas only extended as far as I described above, so it is difficult to judge how many media literacy concepts these lessons might have contained. This discussion group approach thus yielded some intriguing beginnings of lessons.

For their first lesson (see Table 3), which they entitled "Music and Poetry," they clearly focused on including popular culture as a text in the classroom, and they tied it in with traditional curriculum (poetry). Overall, this lesson corresponds loosely with two of Hobbs' key components of media literacy (Hobbs, 1997a). The subgroup participants considered that "individuals negotiate meaning by interacting with messages" (p. 9) by including the essential understanding that "children will be able to identify that different types of music have various meanings." And by examining and comparing music lyrics with poetry, they are asking their students to move toward an understanding that "each form of communication has unique characteristics" (p. 9). However, it is unclear to what extent these points would actually be emphasized.

They simply talked through the second lesson, and it did not contain the details the first lesson did. Their main objective for this particular lesson in mathematics was to have the sixth graders gain an understanding of the value of money. They thought they could accomplish this by constructing a lesson in which their students would be given an amount of money at the beginning of the project that they could spend on items from their favorite catalogs or Websites. The students would be given a short amount of time on a daily basis over a set period of time or until their money was exhausted. Nadia compared this lesson with one she had seen before:

Table 3. Concept-based Unit Template

Unit Title: Music and Poetry

Concepts:
- Understanding artistic expression
- Interpreting music lyrics as poetry
- Creating own lyrics with background music

Essential Understandings/Generalizations:
- Children will be able to show their comprehension of a variety of music through their own creations.
- Children will be able to identify that different types of music have various meanings.
- Children will be able to comprehend that music is a form of poetry.

Guiding Questions:
- What is poetry? What are lyrics?
- Why do you like the music you like?
- Was there a reason/motivation for what you wrote about?
- Have you heard these lyrics? Do you listen to music often?

Enabling Activities:
- Listen to music. Discuss what the artist means.
- Read lyrics and discuss the content (without music).
- Combine both lyrics and music. Discuss. Compare.
- Connect to poetry.
- Write own poetry . . . lyrics (put to selected music).
- Follow up: Distribute same poem to all children and have them put it to music; compare different choices the next day.

Processes and Skills:
- Compare and Contrast.
- Prior exposure to poetry.
- Expression through writing.

Assessment Procedures:
- Observe discussion (use checklist; who's participating?).
- Presentation or looking at their unique piece.
- Class assesses lesson experience.

Materials/Texts:
- Music and CD player.
- Poems and lyrics.

Standard(s) the unit covers:
- English (media literacy, composition, verbal expression, poetry, etc.).
- Science (technology).
- Music (art expression, genre).

I've seen this done with a 5th grade class before, except they planned a trip from Massachusetts to Florida. And they figured out all the hotel costs and the gas and everything from here to there to figure it out. The fifth graders did it, and they planned this big huge thing, and they had the greatest time with it. And it was just the best thing. It was, it was a lot of fun, because then they realized how expensive it is to get from Massachusetts to Florida. It gives them that gratitude too of their parents who take them to Florida all the time and stuff and take them on trips.

With more planning time, perhaps this lesson might have gone in the direction of Hobbs' media literacy component, which states that "messages have economic . . . purposes" (p. 9). However, given their minimal planning, it is too difficult to say; that is, nothing that they discussed hinted at that. Their intention instead leaned toward Nadia's thoughts at the end of the quote above, to have their students understand the value of money, which is not directly related to the general goals of media literacy education.

It is difficult to judge their pedagogical abilities in relation to media literacy by examining these two cases. Perhaps they simply assume that the ideas that "all messages are constructions" or "message are representations of social reality" (Hobbs, 1997, p. 9) will permeate much of their teaching. Given the emerging nature of this content, we can only go on this tertiary examination of how they might consider integrating the media in their classrooms and, as teacher educators, we should consider building from there. They need deeper knowledge of its content along with various strategies for including media literacy beyond the superficial level. Perhaps teacher educators might expose their students to pedagogy within a preservice education course on media literacy education, which would also contain the various elements about which Hobbs writes. Much of this discussion will be continued in the next chapter. For now, however, it is important to consider this subgroup's ideas for making media literacy more visible.

EXPANDING ITS PRESENCE

I think that teaching media and teaching media literacy is important in our schools, whether or not we say it or we just do it, or how we use it. Because children are watching more TV, and children are spending more time on their own at a younger age, that they might be able to benefit from the media when they're watching their television. (Beth, Interview 2, 6/19/01)

As I have written about earlier, there are numerous media literacy proponents in the United States calling for a larger presence of media literacy in our schools, so Beth is not alone in her beliefs. While I did not relay this specific information to the subgroup participants, they were exposed to components of media literacy during the data collection and they did learn from me that media literacy is a part of so many of our states' frameworks. Perhaps all of this explained why, toward the end of the fourth discussion group, Michelle asked: "I just want to know why it's not a part of the regular curriculum, and why it's not taught? I think it's an urgent thing. I think it plays a large role in society." Capitalizing on this, I asked the participants if they could answer Michelle, which reaped some interesting results that are worth fully including here. And it is important to note that the following responses occurred consecutively and without my interruption:

> Nadia: I don't know, personally I think it's because, like we've gone over and over it again, teachers out there don't know. Teachers out there do not know how to teach media literacy. And when you're afraid of something, just like technology or something that's unfamiliar to you or something that you're uncomfortable with, then you're not going to teach it. You're going to shy away from it, until something comes along that says, "this is media literacy; this is what it is; this is how we teach it; this is how you can integrate it in your classroom." And until somebody does that and educates teachers, they're just going to kind of ignore it, because they don't know where to begin. I mean teachers today in the classrooms are overwhelmed and they don't know where to start. And media literacy is a new thing, not new, but it's an unfamiliar territory. And I think it makes people or teachers shy away from it, because they're not familiar with it.

> Beatrice: I think another reason too is that, the whole money issue in schools. Some schools don't have enough money for televisions or for, I know a lot of schools that don't have enough money for computers. You know, just that whole technology and money is, it's incredible. The price for certain equipment, and schools they're running low on money anyway, so they can't afford to have all this type of technology.

> Nadia: Then I think it may also come into the whole controversial stuff. Teachers don't know what to leave out. Teachers don't, you run into a huge thing with parents all the time. The media's another thing that's questionable. You know, "What do you show? What don't you show? What's okay to talk about? What's not okay?" Like we've been talking about, do you share this stuff with a first grade? Do you talk about the commercials and the advertising? So the limits, there are no limits; there are no set standards of what can be shown, what can't be shown and it's risky. It's a risky business when you have parents of 21 children, 25 children, and you have to make everyone happy and not cross any lines. I think that limits it too.

Each of these reasons that Nadia and Beatrice provided—teachers' loose grasp on media literacy pedagogy, a lack of funds, and the media's controversial attributes—highlight their awareness of the problematic nature of integrating media literacy in our schools. But given Michelle's adamant questioning, it seemed important to follow up on this issue during the exit interviews, and it was there that the participants provided their ideas on ways of expanding its presence within K to 12 environments.

They all thought that generally discussing this issue would be the most effective tactic to take in a school where it is lacking. They suggested that it would be important to talk with other teachers, administration, parents, the school board, and Beatrice even mentioned that it might warrant writing a letter to a member of Congress. Their "talk" would be informed by their experiences, which means that most of the subgroup participants, by the end of the study, expressed a desire to incorporate media literacy education within their teaching, though Mary Beth was somewhat tentative because she felt that it was still too far off in her future. Beatrice expressed some trepidation that manifested itself as ambivalence. She felt that the barriers to the inclusion of media literacy as they had discussed were quite high. And she even expressed her troubles with including this visual medium that she feels children are so overexposed to outside of the classroom already. However, in her ambivalence she pointed to its importance as well.

Nadia's statements above suggest the need for media literacy for teachers. My original goal was to investigate media literacy in relation to teacher education. For this reason, within the survey I asked whether they felt that media literacy should be a part of teacher education. Twenty (80%) of the respondents answered yes, while four (16%) were unsure and one (4%) respondent said no. In analyzing the subgroup participants' thoughts on media literacy and teacher education, they fell within the 80%. So I can conclude that both with and without discussion of media literacy, most of the undergraduate participants in my study felt the need for its inclusion in teacher education. And while, with the subgroup, we did not focus on the reasons why it is not already there, in the opening interview Nadia spontaneously expressed her beliefs. "[M]aybe it's because our college professors aren't educated enough on it, on media literacy. Maybe it's because they're lacking on it. Maybe it's trickle down effect; it's a whole hierarchy; maybe nobody knows about it. I don't know." (5/2/01)

While it is clear that these elementary education majors are calling for media literacy in teacher education, (Nadia brings up an important reason of why it is not already there), it also seemed important to discuss their thoughts on ways that it might be incorporated. At the bare minimum, each participant felt that media literacy should be integrated within a course as a chapter or as a seminar. The two courses they mentioned specifically, which could include it, were technology and reading. Only Beatrice expressed the importance of teacher education students taking a course on media analysis, particularly children's media analysis, which emphasizes the value she found in the children's television course she was taking. Within this course, which she envisioned would be structured specifically for education majors, she also felt it would be important to add a component on talking with parents about the media. Nadia gave the most comprehensive analysis and suggestions on this issue during her first interview:

> I feel like it could have been intertwined and showed. They could have taught us how to bring it into the content areas, how to really encourage it, how to teach it. Teach us about it, because obviously, I feel, and I think a lot of people feel, that it was lacking in our childhood. We weren't taught about it K through 12. So maybe they need to start in teaching us about it, so we would have that backing, that background. I feel that it should have been brought up in my curriculum frameworks class, because I took a whole year of curriculum frameworks I and curriculum frameworks II. We went through the whole English strand. We went through the whole math. We went through the whole science. We went through every Massachusetts framework there was, and I went through the English one, and I don't know if we just ignored those columns when we were analyzing it as a class, but I don't remember really hearing about media literacy. (5/2/01)

Teacher educators' lack of knowledge or simply oversight could account for media literacy's absence in teacher education, but with hope, this data might help to begin to remedy this deficiency. Clearly this data show that the interest is there. Knowing where these undergraduate preservice teachers are in terms of their knowledge and skills in relation to media literacy is an important place to begin.

Therefore, in this section I found that this group of preservice teachers believes that they would expand the presence of media literacy at the micro or classroom level and then share their successes and tactics with a wider audience to include other teachers, administration, and parents. I also found that they mostly see the benefits of including media literacy (as they understand it) in teacher education, if only as embedded within an existing course.

In the final chapter I shall elaborate on the larger implications of this study in relation to research, teaching, and policy.

Chapter Seven

Media Literacy and Preservice Elementary Education Teachers: Implications for Policy, Practice and Research

This study was designed to explore the "media worlds" of undergraduates enrolled in elementary education. Its aim was to gain a sense of how deeply and to what extent these students have been exposed to and generally analyze the mass media, to include television, the Internet, advertising, radio, magazines, newspapers, movies, and video games. Beyond the subject matter knowledge, however, I also realized the extent to which these participants might teach this type of material to their future students. My argument has been that their level of content knowledge—to include media literacy subject matter knowledge, pedagogical content knowledge, and curricular knowledge—is modest. And indeed, the data from the survey, interviews and discussion groups show that their self-reported perceptions of media consumption are low, both at home and from their schooling, and along with that, the degree to which they are knowledgeable about media analysis is limited. Their abilities for deep pedagogical and curricular awareness for media literacy compound this deficit.

This book gives an account of the knowledge, skills, beliefs, and experiences of a group of preservice elementary teachers in relation to media literacy. However, the purpose of this book is not to decree particular outcomes as a result of what *these* participants reported about themselves; the findings do not suggest a universality or generalization to all preservice teachers. Rather, perhaps a preferred contribution this study offers is not only *a* profile of some teachers, which itself shows a need for a deepened sense of media literacy content knowledge, but also an emerging conceptual model for the teaching of media literacy in teacher education. I argue that consideration must be given for an expansion of content knowledge for preservice teachers to include various elements of media literacy education, for the media are not only important and compelling in our world, an inclusion of standards for media literacy in 48 of the 50 states also begs its necessity within teacher education.

This study therefore has two major findings on which I elaborate. First, there is a profile of the knowledge, skills, beliefs, and experiences of preservice elementary teachers in relation to the media, popular culture and the teaching of both. Second, using information from the literature on media literacy, much of which comes from the field of communication, and literature in teacher education, I have designed a conceptual model that can act as a springboard for future related policy, practice, and research.

A PROFILE IN REVIEW

The participants in this study reported that the mass media do not play a big role in their lives. Their self-reported perceptions of general media consumption show that they grew up engaging in various types of media less than average and less than many of their peers. As adults, they still viewed themselves as low media consumers. This information is significant when considering their future status as classroom teachers of students who may have higher levels of media consumption. How will they view their future students given this potential difference? The respondents in this study generally viewed media consumption as something that is equated with an escape from reality that is appropriate for periodic indulgence. They said they preferred active pursuits to media consumption. The perception of media consumption as a passive activity or escape from reality further reinforces its submissive veneer; a conceptual outcome they did not acknowledge. Also, with less exposure to the media and popular culture, these future teachers will base many of their judgments on either secondhand information or at least limited sources. Will these future teachers then be as aware as their students of the cultural artifacts that spring forth from popular culture and the media? In our current Information Age, it is perhaps more important than ever to practice seeking out and actively "reading" various sources of popular media texts to evaluate them critically. This is not to suggest that teachers should engage in high(er) levels of media consumption in general; however, I do recommend that teachers have a solid and critical familiarity with the popular culture and media preferences of their students. Peter McLaren emphasizes the pervasive and persuasive nature of the mass media on our culture:

> The representation of reality through corporate sponsorship and pro-
> motional culture has impeded the struggle to establish democratic pub-
> lic spheres and furthered the dissolution of historical solidarities and
> forms of community, accelerating the experience of circular narrative
> time and the postindustrial disintegration of public space. The prolifer-
> ation and phantasmagoria of the image has hastened the death of mod-
> ernist identity structures and has interpolated individuals and groups
> into a world of cyborg citizenry in which 'other' individuals are recon-
> stituted through market imperatives as a collective assemblage of
> "them" read against our "us" (McLaren, 1995, p. 88).

Mass media have thus become an influential epistemology that differs
among individuals by choice and interpretation, and as McLaren might suggest, knowledge and interrogation are necessities.

This group of future teachers described their own school experiences
with the media and popular culture as rather limited. When they were exposed to media texts at school, the idea above that the participation in
media is a passive activity was reinforced by their teachers who neglected
discussing media texts as they might discuss printed texts. In other words,
while an English teacher might examine a writer's use of irony, satire, or
metaphor, he or she might not pause to examine their presence within
media texts. As I stated earlier, their experiences with media at school fell
in line with Hobbs' (1997) notions of media usage for non-educational
purposes; in this case, either for uncritical content reinforcement or even
as a reward. Combining this finding with previous findings on teachers
and their educational biographies (Nespor, 1987), we see that it would be
crucial to spend time within teacher education examining school media biographies to discover the various ways that media are misused, and presented pedagogically to become a form of "hidden curriculum"
(Anderson, 2001). This would better enable new teachers to transcend previous experiences and strive for a smarter integration of media and popular culture in classrooms.

These participants lacked a deep awareness of media aesthetics, or the
techniques that various media makers use to convey their messages to include aspects such as camera angles, lighting, soundtrack/music choices, act-
ing, scriptwriting, etc. This type of knowledge is usually reserved for
communication and/or television/film production majors. It is also knowledge that can be somewhat different for each medium, further emphasizing
its sophistication. Answering the question, what techniques are used to attract my attention, then can require quite a large knowledge base that these
particular preservice elementary teachers are lacking, but could be remedied
with media studies instruction during teacher education.

An advanced aspect of analysis that did emerge in this study was their "reading" of various underlying values put forth in several media texts from advertisements to cartoons to music videos. Some expressed their awareness of certain political values in the story lines and images of the mass media. In our discussion groups, it was obvious that not everyone immediately spotted the underlying values as brought forth by a particular student; however, once a dialogue ensued the ideas were questioned and discussed by all. As I described earlier, during a discussion about advertising and the values it puts forth, Mary Beth was confused. She did not feel that commercials could do such a thing within their short timeframes. Nadia and Beatrice, however, felt differently, and they explained how. Surely Mary Beth left this particular session with a keener eye for spotting underlying values, which perhaps even prompted her later explanation of the values that were present in the cartoon we viewed together. That they had rich discussions and lingering thoughts on this topic further emphasizes the benefits of critical media discussions.

Missing altogether in our sessions was a deep critical awareness of how the economics of the media industry affect the "popular" media we experience. In other words, they never questioned how the conglomeration of media ownership might influence the messages and stories that are sold and told. For deeper analytical awareness what would be needed then is not only further instruction in media economic issues but also more information in the above area of aesthetics, with deepening and further conversations surrounding the socio-historical and political issues of the media and popular culture.

Perhaps by integrating media studies within teacher education, preservice teachers might begin to see the mass media not only as the virulent disease that this particular group sometimes felt it was, but instead they might begin to feel that it is something with which they can and should challenge their future students in complex dialogue. By engaging in the mass media in more mature ways, these preservice teachers might also begin to claim more agency with regard to the dominion they feel it has over us. "Knowledge is power" is a truism that should not escape us here.

Further building on this idea, once these participants gain a deeper level of media studies content knowledge, and hence, appreciation of the media and popular culture, they will be prepared to pass these on to their future students. Currently, however, without this knowledge, their protective instincts are in line with typical teachers (Brookhart, 1992). It seems then that this issue is even more important given their stated propensities toward a preventive outlook, which could combat this part of our culture for children. Initially, time spent problematizing their perceptions of "bad" media might be helpful to recognize that no straight dichotomy is correct here. Media are complex; media are the texts of our lives, and their future students will generally engage in a significant amount of media consumption; therefore, these preservice teachers need to recognize these aspects and not simply shut out all media for the various offenses they feel certain media texts make without informed deliberation.

Within the field of media literacy comes much of the content described above, but for teachers, there are the added tasks of knowing how to translate the subject of media literacy for students in various ways and knowing where to find appropriate curricula. Most of these participants did not realize the scope of media literacy as forwarded by its proponents. However, according to Tyner (1998), even the proponents are rarely clear in defining and explicating the pursuits within media literacy. In this case the preservice teachers were completely unaware of this term prior to participating in this study. This unawareness explains their general inability, at least early on, to define media literacy in the robust way that it is generally understood. I will elaborate on how their more complex definitions at the end attest to the methods I utilized as not only research but also pedagogical tools.

Prior to this intervention I found that they generally neglected to consider "communication" or media production as a component of media literacy, which I liken to teaching kids to read, but not to write. If left without the instruction and exposure to media production, some students *may* go on to discover their abilities to tell stories through visuals. However, most will not, which is fundamental when considering and comparing it again with print literacy in which some scholars strongly forward the notion that writing enhances reading. And so it is the same here where a total consideration for the various parts of the definition of media literacy—access, analyze, evaluate, *and* communicate—is crucial.

What emerged quite clearly in this research was that the desire for learning more about media literacy education was rather strong in these participants. True, the particular motivations varied, from Mary Beth's interest in learning more about production aspects to Beatrice's curiosity about discussing the media with parents, but the overall corresponding urge to know more about media literacy shone through. Both Tyner (1998) and Considine (2000a) acknowledge that media literacy education has generally expanded at the grassroots or teacher level, which perhaps attests to the potential power of an individual teacher's interests. Here these preservice teachers attest to their intuitive interests in this field, not only as one that interests them for various personal reasons but also as a field that they generally feel is important for children.

During this research project, skill at operating media technology dominated these participants' concerns for including media literacy in classrooms. Teachers not knowing how to utilize technology across various platforms, teachers not knowing how to program a VCR or use editing equipment were prioritized as barriers to successful media literacy. And, as I have written, this skills-based approach to media literacy is limiting in its neglect of the various socio-cultural/analytical aspects of the media, and more importantly here in this meta-discussion of media literacy for teachers, their minimal concern for the pedagogy and curriculum of media literacy shows their naïveté. This is not to say, however, that they did not acknowledge the importance of the pedagogical and curricular aspects. They did indeed, and of course, they also recognized how limited teachers (including themselves) are in these aspects as well. Considering the dimensions of Shulman's (1986) suggestions for teachers' content knowledge, there is much missing in terms of this field for teachers.

These participants' emerging pedagogical abilities for the wide field of media literacy education came through in the case methods during the second discussion group. Not only was their grasp of discussing the media and popular culture with students varied and uncertain, their ideas for including it in their teaching were lacking. However, it was important to gauge nevertheless, for there may be assumptions by teacher educators that given the nature of popular media texts, young teachers might naturally include them in their teaching. But again, I must reconvene the complexities of this field. To include media literacy in classrooms by the standards of a critical pedagogue, multiple readings must occur and be appreciated, with "emancipatory agendas" particularly being forwarded (Weaver & Daspit, 1999), and additionally, as I explained above, there must be a space for and education in the communication with media. This specified pedagogical content knowledge then may best take place during teacher education.

Interestingly again, much like Tyner (1998) and Considine (2000a), these preservice teachers see that the expansion of this field can occur at the grassroots level, in their case within their own future classrooms. The dominant view held by these participants was that they would try to continue educating themselves about this field, but they did not speak about grand systemic ways for its expansion. Instead, they felt that by their education and teaching experiences with it, their own work might help it to spread. Perhaps one could view this as preservice teacher idealism, but in this case, it interestingly seems to correspond with its growth worldwide thus far.

Going along with my personal agenda, their beliefs in relation to the inclusion of media literacy in teacher education provided various insights.

In reflecting on their own teacher education experiences and this emerging field, they generally felt that it should be more ever present by being included within various courses such as technology or literacy/language arts methods. But in considering Beatrice's experiences alone, having taken and valued a communication course on children's television, it seems clear that a course such as this, as she suggests, taught in teacher education would be quite valuable.

MEDIA LITERACY IN TEACHER EDUCATION

While a course for preservice teachers can and should include elements of children's media, additional elements need to be considered as well. This leads to a discussion of the emerging conceptual model I am forwarding as a springboard from this research, which would ideally not only lead to the inclusion of media literacy education in more teacher education programs but as well to further research that could examine this issue in more detail and, more importantly, provide more of a solid foundation for classroom practice.

The model below (see Figure 2) is in the shape of a spiral triangle that represents not only the three components of teacher content knowledge that Shulman calls for but also in this particular case, an expansion on his categories for this specific subject. The spiral triangle contains various elements that I feel have emerged from this overall study, which are important for a teacher's deepening knowledge base in media literacy education with a consideration of teaching. And while it may seem that these elements are prioritized in a building-block manner—that is, one component is required before another—this is not necessarily the case here, as I see each of these elements as comprising a total composition of what is necessary for preservice teachers learning media literacy. Additionally, I purposefully have not completely filled in this expanding triangle, for I believe that this allows for others to either individualize new areas as per localized contexts and/or to consider new elements that will come with changes in our Information Age with the main objective being a deepened sense of content knowledge for teachers.

In terms of subject matter knowledge, I believe that teachers need to be able to read and interpret broader contextual issues of historical, economic, political and aesthetic concern with regard to the media and popular culture. Each of these elements can play a big role in determining various interpretations of media texts, and each requires a distinct and broad knowledge base. Preservice teachers studying media literacy content also need to get to a place whereby they will seek out a variety of media texts for cross-comparative analyses. They should be able to make and acknowledge varying interpretations of a media text without allowing for "the abandonment of emancipatory agendas, ethical imperatives, or radical democratic projects" (Weaver and Daspit, 1999, p. xix). Preservice teachers should be able to tell a story with pictures, use editing equipment, build Websites, and operate other various media communication systems. They need to be able to detect omissions within a media text, whether of a value or aesthetic nature. They should be able to problematize and discuss issues around media power to aim toward ideas for self and citizen empowerment. And preservice teachers should be familiar with a basic history and current status of the media, specifically children's media, and media literacy education in an international context.

In terms of curricular knowledge, undergraduate education students should be exposed to various existing media literacy curricula such as videos, textbooks, and Websites. Additionally, they should be familiar not only with general media studies curricula but also curricula within potential strands in which media literacy might easily be embedded, such as health, social studies, and language arts. Finally, these participants would want to be familiar with curricula within the critical literacy field for it may often and easily connect with content material for media literacy.

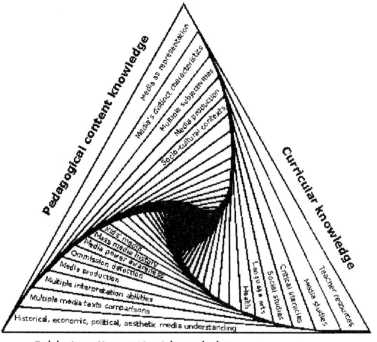

Figure 2. Media Literacy Content Knowledge

Finally, for the strand of pedagogical content knowledge, my research suggests that preservice teachers should be able to teach a variety of concepts, which are related to and include many of the areas above. To reiterate from chapter two, Cassandra Book (1989) wrote, "How teachers understand the disciplinary knowledge and how they represent that content to students through the individual pedagogical content decisions and the broader curricular decisions they make affects the nature of knowledge students will come to have about the discipline" (p. 320). Here it is also possible that certain content items should be considered on a more specific basis depending on the grade level the teacher will teach. Generally speaking, however, when all teachers are discussing media and popular culture with their students, they should consider making a note of the various historical, economic, political and aesthetic aspects surrounding a media text. It is also important for teachers to be able to get across the concept that the media are representations of reality. This may be accomplished differently depending on the age of the child. Next, it is important to be able to distinguish and teach about the distinct characteristics of different types of media, which might be accomplished during different grades. For example, perhaps a different medium might be focused on exclusively for a particular grade level. Teachers should also be able to teach students the idea that there are multiple subjectivities within media texts, which might be a concept that is saved for later grades. Finally, all teachers should have the pedagogical content knowledge to teach the skills involved in various types of media production, to include not only the mechanics but as well the aesthetics for telling a compelling story with pictures. And so again, perhaps this area is most important in this research process so as to differentiate this course from a general course in media literacy. Shulman proclaimed that pedagogical content knowledge is "the particular form of content knowledge that embodies the aspects of content most germane to its teachability. . . . In a word, the ways of representing and formulating the subject that make it comprehensible to others" (p. 9).

IMPLICATIONS FOR POLICY

The above developing conceptual design helps to forward this field of media literacy in terms of teacher education policy. In their rubric for content knowledge NCATE states that the highest level (target) for "teacher candidates [should include] in-depth knowledge of the subject matter that they plan to teach as described in professional, state and institutional standards. They [should] demonstrate their knowledge through inquiry, critical analysis and synthesis of the subject" (NCATE, 2002, p. 17). Many of these goals are apparent within this developing field. For example, media literacy is a "subject matter" within many state standards. Media literacy also easily encourages learning through inquiry, critical analysis, and a synthesis of various subjects. Additionally, there are conceptual elements of media literacy within the NCATE standard (4) on diversity. Specifically, NCATE suggests that teacher "candidates learn to contextualize teaching and to draw upon representations from the students' own experiences and knowledge . . . [as well as] to challenge students toward cognitive complexity and engage all students. . . ." (p. 32). Perhaps at a national policy level, NCATE standards might one day address specific references to media literacy education.

Once again, I have placed an emphasis on the pervasiveness of media in our culture and as a part of students' experiences and knowledge. I have also impressed upon the fact that we need to challenge this knowledge, which may easily be taken for granted. Policy for media literacy already exists in 48 out of 50 states. And "[a]s Texas begins introducing testing in media literacy, one wonders whether the process will support or subvert the movement" (Considine, 2002, p. 13). Considine struggles with the motivation of media literacy's advancement in our schools today because of the strong accountability movement, for rote memorization and the recall of facts are completely antithetical to the principles of media literacy; yet its inclusion in national policy gives it a certain credibility. His resolution, which agrees with me, is for teachers learning about this field to look beyond the mandates and "personalize the process" (Considine, 2002, p. 14).

Media literacy can also help to promote teacher education that strives for social justice. In his 2001 article entitled, "The value of critical perspectives in teacher education," Landon Beyer describes teacher education that centers on topics related to social justice, equality, and democratic values:

> By creating both courses and field experiences for prospective teachers that deal with issues of social class, race, ethnicity, gender and sexual orientation, teacher educators may link broader political, ideological, and social issues with the concrete realities of schools. Teachers who embody these orientations will intervene in the lives of their students so as to help construct with them futures that are personally rewarding, socially responsible, and morally compelling. (p. 151)

Media literacy again could help forward these pursuits, as its underlying aims are all about political and social issues. If it were embedded in the curricular policies of such institutions, it would easily help to promote the goals of social justice teacher education.

IMPLICATIONS FOR PRACTICE

According to a 1999 study by the Kaiser Family Foundation, "the typical American child spends an average of more than 38 hours a week—nearly five and a half hours a day—consuming media outside of school" (Weitz, 1999, p. 1). As I stated in the problem section in chapter one, this should make the study of the media and popular culture mandatory in schools. How can our daily classroom practice continue to ignore such an ever-present part of our students' worlds? Compound this pervasiveness with the current limited focus on media studies in teacher education and there is clearly an opportunity for an expansion in the practice of teachers in our future.

Knowing that teachers are already overloaded with new teaching demands, how is it that I dare suggest the inclusion of yet another new field? The answer, given the above statistic, is that students are already equipped with a particular content base that teachers can use to capitalize on teachable moments. Additionally, a lot of this field includes, as I explained above, consideration for historical, economic, political and aesthetic contextual information. This allows for the field of media literacy to be similar to the field of multicultural education in that it can and should spread across a variety of disciplines, but additionally, it can be a distinct discipline as well, perhaps particularly in the case of aesthetic background. Further,

> [B]y contributing multiple perspectives based on diverse cultural readings of popular culture texts, students who are inundated with mass media forms also bring a great deal of common prior knowledge of mass media narratives. . . . Thus, sophisticated readings of familiar texts, coupled with experiences in media-making, are powerful tools for teachers of diverse classrooms. (Tyner, 1998, p. 166)

And so there are various ways in which media literacy and multiculturalism have a symbiotic relationship. Again, this is an important implication for the growing diversity existing in U.S. schools.

IMPLICATIONS FOR RESEARCH

Research of this sort, which deals with theories from education, literacy and communication, is still somewhat rare, yet perhaps likely to become more common in the future. Kathleen Tyner (1998) discusses Walter Ong's concept of "secondary orality," which merges oral and print cultures in electronic forms. She sees this merger as promising in that it is promoting "a convergence of communication theory and literacy theory . . . [which] has the added bonus of offering multiple paths of literacy for the learner, who may be predisposed to aural, visual, or textual modes" (p. 57), with an end result of promoting more learning opportunities for all students.

My chosen research methodology also came with implications for further examination and potential replication. In her last interview, Nadia spoke about this research experience as one that pushed them forward in their learning:

> I think that I learned a lot from the people [in this research project]. I thought that was really important . . . because it made me realize that there were only five of us in that room. There were only five of us talking and telling and sharing ideas, and still there were five totally different things going on. I mean we had a lot in common about the way we saw the media, but like, our history growing up made me realize that there's five of us, and I'm going to have a classroom of 25 kids. And imagine the different home lives that they're having, the different media exposure, you know? The different ways that they're getting it and different amounts, that was really interesting to hear other people, me, who didn't have any media, then Mary Beth, who had lots of media. And um, seeing the difference[s]; wow, I'm really going to have to prepare for the different, kind of like doing the different levels of learning. It's the same way with media. It's a wide range of exposure and stuff. (Nadia, Interview 2, 6/15/01)

I will end here with what I see as an important legacy of this particular project; that is, the particular methodology I utilized. As Nadia described above, this project became more than just an opportunity for me to collect data on their knowledge, skills, beliefs, and experiences with the mass media, popular culture, and media literacy. It also resulted in an empowering experience for the participants. I can also combine this sentiment with the data that emerged showing the growth that took place in their ideas about media literacy from the beginning of the research to the end. The data collection process became a sort of intervention for the participants, and thus was not only a methodology but also pedagogy. For this complex reason I struggled for some time to name exactly what I did. I engaged in many conversations with various colleagues who are well versed in methodological issues, and no one person could help lay an exact claim to this type of particular process. Mostly I identified many of the things it was not. It was not "action research," because the participants did not have the opportunity to make any particular changes in their organization or structure (Stringer, 1999). Though it seemed to be an intervention, it was not quasi-experimental research given the types of methods I utilized; and so the discussions went with my ending choices being what appeared in the third chapter.

It is imperative that we seek to produce more critically minded and democratic citizens during this Information Age in which much of what we need to thrive is mediated through multiple mediums with certain voices being louder and more ever-present than others. One of the best ways for our citizenry to become better informed and more critical about their surroundings is through education, and so teachers tend to hold a lot of responsibility. As the findings in this study suggest, our future teachers need to be able to analyze, converse about, and produce mass media, and teach media literacy education. Perhaps future studies focusing on preservice and in-service education, as well as media literacy learning/application with children might help to further validate and move this important field forward. Hopefully teacher educators will join more steadily in the process to increase the numbers of teachers who are media literate and can teach it.

Appendix A
Media Literacy Survey and Results

Thank you very much for participating in the following survey on media. "Media" in this survey means TV, movies, videos, magazines, radio, newspapers, video games, and the Internet. I am interested to know what future teachers' histories and current knowledge of media are, so that teacher preparation programs can respond appropriately. This survey is the first part of a larger research study (my dissertation for my Ph.D. at Boston College) about preservice teachers and media literacy. I am looking to recruit approximately 8 to 10 volunteer participants for the next phase, which will involve interviews with me and group sessions where we will watch and discuss various media products. Participants interested in this phase should contact me directly at sflores@xxxxx for more details. (There will be incentives for your participation!) Thanks again!

Instructions: There are 4 sections to this survey. First, you will answer questions about your media past at home and then at school. Next, you will answer questions about your current media usage. Third, you will answer questions regarding your skills with media and teaching the media. And finally, you will answer questions about your general knowledge of media.

Results based on 25 responses.

YOUR MEDIA PAST—HOME (2–17)

1. The average U.S. child (age 2–17) spends nearly 3 hours per day watching TV. Was your TV viewing . . .
   52% (13) About average
   40% (10) Less than average
   8% (2) More than average

2. When it came to TV, my parents set limits on my viewing time and programs that were
   72% (18) Somewhat restrictive
   20% (5) Very restrictive
   8% (2) Not restrictive at all

3. How much did you listen to the radio on a daily basis?
   56% (14) 1–2 hours
   24% (6) 3 or more hours
   20% (5) Less than 1 hour

4. I read the newspaper
   64% (16) 1 or more times a week but not daily
   28% (7) Never
   8% (2) Daily

5. I went to the movies
   56% (14) About once a month
   28 % (7) About once a week
   16% (4) About once a year

6. I played with video games
   44% (11) Less than 1 hour
   40% (10) Never
   12% (3) 1–2 hours
   4% (1) 3 or more hours

7. I was on the Internet daily for
   56% (14) Never
   24% (6) Less than 1 hour
   16% (4) 1–2 hours
   4% (1) 3 or more hours

YOUR MEDIA PAST—SCHOOL (K-12)

8. How often did you watch videos/films at school?
   56% (14) About once a month
   28% (7) About once a semester
   12% (3) About once a week
   4% (1) Never

9. I watched videos at school as a reward when our class behaved well.
   48% (12) About once a semester
   32% (8) Never
   20% (5) About once a month

10. I watched videos at school that corresponded with our class topic.
    48% (12) About once a month
    40% (10) About once a semester
    12% (3) About once a week
11. When I watched videos at school my teachers discussed how the video was made.
    64% (16) Never
    36% (9) Sometimes
12. I made media (ex. videos, radio shows, etc.) at school.
    56% (14) Never
    36% (9) About once a semester
    8% (2) About once a week
13. I used the internet at school.
    44% (11) Never
    32% (8) About once a semester
    24% (6) About once week
14. Media literacy was a part of my K–12 education.
    40% (10) Not sure
    32% (8) Yes
    28% (7) No

YOUR CURRENT MEDIA USAGE

15. I currently watch TV
    68% (17) Less than 3 hours a day
    20% (5) About 3 hours a day
    8% (2) Never
    4% (1) More than 3 hours a day
16. How many magazines do you read regularly in a month?
    76% (19) 1–2
    12% (3) 0
    12 (3) 3 or more
17. How much do you currently listen to the radio on a daily basis?
    40% (10) 3 or more hours
    32% (8) Less than 1 hour
    20% (5) 1–2 hours
    8% (2) Never
18. I read the newspaper
    56% (14) 1 or more times per week but not daily
    40% (10) Never
    4% (1) Daily

19. I go to the movies
    48% (12) About once a month
    24% (6) About once a year
    16% (4) About once a week
    12% (3) Never
20. I play with video games
    88% (22) Never
    4% (1) Less than 1 hour a day
    4% (1) 3 or more hours a day
    4% (1) 1–2 hours a day
21. I am on the Internet
    64% (16) Less than 3 hours a day
    28% (7) More than 3 hours a day
    8% (2) About 3 hours a day

YOUR MEDIA SKILLS

22. I know how to program a VCR.
    88% (22) Yes
    8% (2) Not Sure
    4% (1) No
23. I know how to operate a video camera.
    92% (23) Yes
    4% (1) Not Sure
    4% (1) No
24. I know how to use video editing equipment.
    52% (13) No
    24% (6) Not Sure
    24% (6) Yes
25. I know how to create a PowerPoint presentation.
    80% (20) Yes
    12% (3) No
    8% (2) Not Sure
26. I know how to build and launch a website.
    40% (10) Yes
    36% (9) Not Sure
    24% (6) No
27. I feel prepared to teach kids how to tell a story with video.
    44% (11) Yes
    36% (9) Not Sure
    20% (5) No

28. I feel prepared to teach kids how to edit a video.
72% (18) No
24% (6) Not Sure
4% (1) Yes
29. I feel prepared to teach kids how to build a website.
52% (13) No
24% (6) Not Sure
24% (6) Yes

YOUR GENERAL MEDIA KNOWLEDGE

30. I understand what media literacy means.
48% (12) Not Sure
48% (12) Yes
4% (1) No
31. Camera angles can make a character seem more or less important.
92% (23) Yes
8% (2) Not Sure
32. Advertisers market their products differently to different demographic groups.
92% (23) Yes
8% (2) Not Sure
33. Saturday morning network TV commercials are different from Wednesday morning network TV commercials.
84% (21) Yes
16% (4) Not Sure
34. Media shape U.S. culture.
76% (19) Yes
20% (5) Not Sure
4% (1) No
35. U.S. culture shapes the media.
60% (15) Yes
24% (6) Not Sure
16% (4) No
36. U.S. culture and the media influence each other more or less equally.
64% (16) Yes
20% (5) Not Sure
16% (4) No
37. I have studied the media in my college coursework.
64% (16) No
32% (8) Yes

4% (1) Not Sure

38. I wish I knew more about media literacy.
    79.2% (19) Yes
    12.5% (3) Not Sure
    8.3% (2) No

39. I have the knowledge and skills to teach kids about media analysis.
    43.5% (10) Not Sure
    43.5% (10) No
    13% (3) Yes

40. In helping my students become media literate, I feel . . .
    83.3% (20) Somewhat prepared
    12.5% (3) Prepared
    4.2% (1) Not prepared at all

41. Media literacy should be a part of teacher education.
    80% (20) Yes
    16% (4) Not Sure
    4% (1) No

Individual Interview One

QUESTIONS

(Remind participants what is meant by "media" for this study.)

- Why did you volunteer for this research project?
- Before I introduced this project and you took the survey, had you heard of media literacy? Where? Under what circumstances? How?
- How do you define media literacy? Do you feel as though you're media literate? If so, how did it happen?
- Tell me about your media habits when you were a kid, growing up at home? (i.e., how much TV, movies, magazines, Internet, video games, radio did you utilize?)
- Tell me about your media habits at school. Under what circumstances and to what extent did you analyze/interpret/understand media? Did you make media? What kind? How? Did you enjoy it?
- What media do you prefer now? What's your favorite TV show, movie, music group/singer, Internet site, radio station, etc.? Why? How often do you participate in media? Why so little/so much?
- What media (particular programs or people) do you like least? Why?
- How do determine that a piece of news is accurate? That is, how do you decide what to believe?
- Have you discussed media issues/popular culture here at your college? How so? Why? Did you get something out of it?

- Do you think it's a good idea to bring media/popular culture in the elementary classroom? Why or why not? Be specific—what is appropriate in an elementary classroom?

- Can media literacy thrive in a standards-based environment like we have here in MA now? Should it be a part of the MCAS? If so, how?

- Let's say media literacy does become a part of elementary curriculum, what is needed by teachers to teach kids about it? (i.e., curriculum materials, equipment, teacher knowledge, etc.) Should teachers keep up with youth media? Is this important? Why?

- Was media literacy a part of your teacher education? Would it have been helpful if media literacy were a part of your teacher education? How could media literacy be a part of teacher education?

- If we draw a parallel between print literacy and media literacy, and say that if we are literate in print, we practice it by reading and writing, how do you practice your media literacy skills?

Discussion Group One

QUESTIONS

- What did you learn the other day from our conversation/interview?
- Have you thought about anything we discussed in particular? *Metacognitive*
- On the survey, a group said that they felt confident to teach kids how to tell a story with video; let's expand that to pictures and tell me how you would do this? *Pedagogical question—skills*
- Also on the survey there were a couple of questions about advertising and demographics (re-read the questions from the survey); tell me more about what you know about this in more than one medium. *The business of media—knowledge*
- Talk about your beliefs as far as U.S. culture and the media/popular culture—which one is more influential to the other? *Media impact—analysis/knowledge*
- Do you think that media/popular culture is more good or more bad for us? *Personal perceptions and the potential to affect teaching—knowledge/beliefs*
- When does media influence begin in terms of identity formation and how long do you think it lasts? *Media analysis—knowledge*
- Why don't you guys ever watch PBS or other channels that show "educational" media? *Access*
- Do you know what "alternative" media is? *Access*
- Do you think that media literacy always needs to be called media literacy directly? (i.e., some of you had aspects of media literacy in

classes before, and this came out in your talk, yet in general you didn't count this when we spoke, why?) *Self-awareness— Knowledge*

- Has anyone ever seen professional media being made? *Media analysis—communication*
- What more do you wish you knew about media literacy? *Knowledge*

Appendix D
Media Survey for Sixth Grade Language Arts Students

Hi!

My friend Steph is writing a *really* long essay about how teachers use media (TV, movies, music, commercials . . .) when they are teaching kids. Before she begins, Steph needs to gather some information about what media is popular with kids your age.

If you want to help Steph, please fill in the following survey with the first idea that comes into your head. I may use some of this information too when I am teaching you.

Thanks!

What is your favorite:

Movie? _____

TV show? _____

Song? _____

Singer or music group? _____

Clothes store or store at the mall? _____

Commercial? _____

Website? _____

Is there anything else you'd like to tell Steph (or me)? Use the back of this sheet to write us a short note.

Discussion Group Three

SIGNAL TO NOISE QUESTIONS

Group #3–May 14, 2001

Before viewing the video *Signal to Noise: Life with Television, Watching TV Watching Us* (approximately one hour) I want to give them the following questions to think about while they're viewing it for discussion afterwards. I think I actually might print up these questions so they can jot down notes for each question. First I'll introduce the video briefly, then we'll read through the questions. I'll ask them to jot down notes while they're viewing the video, but additionally, I'll give them time after the video to elaborate in writing before we discuss the questions together. Here are the questions:

- What surprised you in this video? What new things did you learn? *Self-awareness knowledge*
- How was their analysis different from your own? *Self-awareness knowledge*
- How was their analysis like your own? *Self-awareness knowledge*
- How does watching something like this enhance your skepticism or negativity about the media? *Media analysis*
- How does watching something like this enhance your positive feelings about the media? *Media analysis*
- Do you see this as being good for use in a classroom? If so, in what context/content and with what sorts of extended assignments or lessons? *PCK*

Appendix F
Discussion Group Four

WEBSITE QUESTIONS

Group #4–May 17, 2001

Part One:

Explore the following Website produced by the University of Oregon on your own for approximately a half-hour and jot down notes below on things that interest you and/or you wish to explore further at a later date.

Http://interact.uoregon.edu/medialit/MLR/home/index.html

Part Two:

Construct a set of standards for elementary students on media literacy.

Construct a set of standards for teacher education students on media literacy.

Individual Interview Two

QUESTIONS

June 2001

- Have you talked about this project with anyone? If so, what have you said and/or how have you described it?
- On a few occasions, you all said that teachers need skills in media, but since it seems that the five of you have basic skills in terms of media usage, I might assume that most college-aged people also do, what would/might be useful for you to learn in a college course on media literacy?
- Should a video be paused in a classroom? When and why? Is it okay just to show a part of a video?
- Have you thought of any other potential content-area lessons where media or media literacy can be integrated?
- On page 9 (discussion group 4), Nadia discusses how kids need to know the relevance/importance of media literacy. Why do you think this is so? And, how is it that you can *show* its relevance as opposed to *telling* its relevance to students?
- On a few occasions during the discussion groups you guys talked about how media is different today than it was when you were kids. Do you think this? If so, why is this significant for you as a future teacher? Is it?
- How would you talk with a student who proudly comes to tell you about his/her favorite music group, TV show, movie, etc, and you find it objectionable?
- Some of you said you didn't "get" that episode of "Dexter's Lab." Do adults really need to understand or "get" kids' media?

- What should you, as a teacher, suggest to parents so their kids will watch less TV and/or watch it more responsibly?
- When is it that we are skeptical or critical of what media we experience? When is it that we should be skeptical or critical of what media we experience?
- In our discussions and in the "Signal to Noise" video I heard that TV is an escape. What is it an escape from? What do you think about this?
- What do you think is significant about the mixture of business and media?
- In the standards for teachers that you came up with, Beth suggested that teachers should be free of bias when teaching the media, and everyone seemed to agree. What do you mean by this exactly? Do you think it's possible to be totally bias-free? And what are the different ways that bias might affect the students you teach?
- In various places throughout the transcripts I noticed that you all expressed ambivalent feelings when it came to various aspects of the media (i.e., you thought that TV as an escape was both good and bad, as well as identifying and learning from characters). Do you feel this way? If so, how can you deal with this with your future students?
- In the fourth discussion group, Michelle asked why media literacy wasn't more widespread in schools. You all gave various answers such as a lack of money, fear by teachers since it's a new content area, and media's controversial nature. Michelle also said she thinks that we need to fight for it. How could you see yourself fighting for it? How could you see others fighting for it?
- How do you now define media literacy?
- What have you learned about yourself as a result of what we've talked about?

Nadia questions:

- On a few occasions you mentioned that media in lessons must have a purpose (for example, you explained that when you played the "Oregon Trail" in elementary school, you didn't recognize its significance or connection to anything else you were learning). My question for you is, do you think this idea of purposeful lessons could extend beyond media? That is, is it just the insertion of media that makes lessons without purpose?

- On page 7 (discussion group 1), you imply an "us versus them" mentality in terms of people and the media. Do you feel this way? What do you think of that now? What are the implications?
- What was so wrong about the parents bribing their kids not to watch television? What's an alternative for parents to use so their kids won't watch a lot of TV?
- On page 8 (discussion group 3), clarify what you meant by this?
- On page 8 (discussion group 4) you say "maybe teachers need to know the limits of how much they should provide to their students. Like the stuff that should be left out." What do you mean by this?

Beth questions:

- How influential do you think the third grade teacher was on you and/or your family?
- Read her quote on page 7 (discussion group 1) and ask her to elaborate on it. Should media literacy really be taught differently in different school districts? If so, how should it be different specifically?
- On page 9 (discussion group 4), you said that teachers should know how to apply different kinds of media to different kinds of curriculum. What do you mean by this?
- In the last discussion group I asked if you could draw a parallel between media literacy and another content area. You said that for you, it most closely relates to technology. Can you expand on what you mean by this? (page 9 and 10)

Beatrice questions:

- Do you think your late entry into computers contributed to your current low usage of them?
- Why do you say that "Dharma and Greg" influences you? (interview 1, page 7)
- When you talked about how stuff in the media reflects in kids' play and their speech, and that it's important for teachers to know about this, why? So what? How does that help a teacher teach better?
- You said you were shocked at the businessman's statement in the video when he said that he's not in the business to educate; schools are. Why were you so surprised at this?

- On page 9/10 (discussion group 3), when Nadia asked why U.S. TV is broadcast abroad, yet we do not see foreign TV, you said, "because we have Hollywood." What did you mean by this exactly? That is, what do you believe the implications are of our Hollywood?
- Tell me what you wrote about for your final exam question in your children's TV class.

Michelle questions:

- Did you change your major yet?
- In your interview you explain that teachers need knowledge in order to teach about media literacy. What kind of knowledge did you mean exactly? (p. 10)

Mary Beth questions:

- Initially you thought that being media literate meant being exposed to a lot of media. Do you still feel this way after our discussions?

Appendix H
Letter of Consent

Dear Preservice Elementary Education Major:

Currently, I am completing my doctoral studies at Boston College in the Lynch School of Education's Curriculum and Instruction Department under the direct supervision of Dr. Tom Keating. As a final part of my degree I must complete a dissertation, which involves original research. The project I have chosen is entitled, "Preservice Teachers and Media Literacy Education: Their Knowledge, Skills, and Experience."

Briefly, I want to find out how undergraduates in the elementary education major understand media for themselves, as well as for their future students and their teaching careers. Your experiences, opinions, and insights are thus crucial for this project and the future of media literacy education in the United States.

The survey that you so kindly completed was the first phase of my study. The next parts include 1–3 casual individual interview/conversations with me that might last up to one hour each. In these we will talk about your media history and your insights into media today and the teaching of media to elementary-aged students. Additionally, I would like to gather small groups together to experience media, whether at a movie, on-line, on a video, etc., and then have a conversation. I would like to videotape all of these sessions, but my immediate plan does not include showing the video to anyone. You will be assigned a pseudonym as soon as you agree to voluntarily participate, and no identifying information will be given to your school or anyone else, for that matter. I'm hoping that our time together will only last this semester if your schedule permits, but I'm willing to extend into the summer and travel to you at that time. For now, my schedule is wide-open for this project, and we will meet at your convenience.

Your participation in this research is voluntary. If you feel that some material we may cover is uncomfortable to you, you are free to drop out at any time. The benefits of the research for you would be the opportunity to engage in an experience that will enhance your future teaching. Also, expect to be treated to these media events, as I will pay, and as well, we'll have food during the various group sessions. Additionally, I hope we will have fun just chatting about your media interests, as I plan to share with you my own as it is appropriate. Finally, feel free to contact me at any time via e-mail sflores@xxxxxx or by telephone (H) 978-xxx-xxxx (cell) 617-xxx-xxxx if you have questions or concerns about the project anytime along the way. Also, if you wish to contact my advisor Dr. Tom Keating, his e-mail is keatingt@xxxxxx. When I complete this some time next year, I would be more than happy to provide you with a summary of the findings at your request.

Sincerely,

INFORMED CONSENT FORM

You have been invited to participate in a research project being conducted by Stephanie A. Flores. Participation is voluntary. The purpose of this research is to improve our understanding of media literacy and preservice teachers.

    I, _____ agree to participate in the above research by consenting to meet with Stephanie for casual videotaped interviews and discussion groups about my media history, my thoughts about media in general, and my ideas regarding the teaching of media to my future students.

    I understand that any written, oral, or visual presentation that may be developed will be presented in such a way that my anonymity will be protected.

    I understand that my participation is voluntary and that I may withdraw at any time from the research. I am also free to ask any questions concerning the research during or after my participation. Furthermore, I understand that Stephanie will pay for any media expenses incurred, and there will not be any direct academic benefits to my involvement.

    In signing this form, I agree to participate in the research under the conditions stated above.

_____
Signature of Participant/Date

_____
Printed Name

_____

_____

_____
Telephone Number(s) at school, home, etc. (indicate which one)

_____
Date you will move home

_____
Home address

Appendix I
Letter of participation

September 7, 2001

Dear [Participant]:

I am writing this letter in appreciation for your volunteer participation in my dissertation research for my Ph.D. at Boston College's Lynch School of Education. I am extremely grateful for the many hours that you gave up in order to meet with me at the end of the spring semester 2001 and into the summer. Not only that, however, your insights and contributions within the interviews and discussion groups are adding rich layers to my dissertation analysis and writing. As I explained to you at various times during our meetings, the field of media literacy is still in its infancy in the United States and even younger within teacher education. Your thoughts and comments are hopefully creating part of a foundation for a future discipline. My study, entitled "Preservice Teachers and Media Literacy Education: Their Knowledge, Skills and Experience" is aimed at bringing this field to the attention of scholars in teacher education so they can begin to consider the implications of including elements of media literacy within the field of teacher education. Hopefully, by my wise use of your words, they will take notice and understand how undergraduates understand and appreciate this burgeoning field.

Enclosed is a list of media literacy references for you to keep and hopefully utilize one day. I wish you the best of luck in your education career. I know after talking with you extensively that you will work hard to always seek the best ways of educating your students. Please do not hesitate to contact me at any time for further information on media literacy or the field of education in general.

With deep gratitude,

Stephanie A. Flores

New England Board of Higher Education

Pre-doctoral Fellow

Notes

NOTES TO CHAPTER ONE

1. NCATE is an accreditation council for teacher education programs with its own set of standards (www.ncate.org). Within the elementary language arts standards (p. 6 and p. 70-2b), viewing is one of the skills that new teachers must understand and be able to apply in the classroom. Additionally, within elementary instruction (p. 7-3e) NCATE suggests that teachers be able to "use their knowledge and understanding of effective verbal, nonverbal and media communication techniques to foster active inquiry, collaboration and supportive interaction in the elementary classroom." Finally, within this same section on page 36 it states that "Candidates (should) understand communication theory . . . model effective communication strategies in conveying ideas and information and in asking questions (e.g., monitoring the effects of messages; restating ideas, and drawing connections; using visual aural, and kinesthetic cues, being sensitive to nonverbal cues given and received) . . . candidates (should) know (also) how to use a variety of media communication tools . . ."

NOTES TO CHAPTER TWO

1. Channel One is a school/business partnership, offering schools free media equipment in exchange for mandatory student viewing of a daily news show with commercials.

Bibliography

ACME. (2004). Frequently Asked Questions. Retrieved February 27, 2004, from http://www.acmecoalition.org/about2.html#faq.

Alvermann, D.E., & Hagood, M.C. (2000). Critical media literacy: Research, theory, and practice in "New Times." *The Journal of Educational Research, 93*(3), 193–205.

Anderson, S. (2002). *A critical look at media literacy practice.* Unpublished doctoral dissertation, University of St. Thomas, Minneapolis, MN.

Anderson, S. (2002, April 5). Media literacy in the U.S. Message posted to Media-l electronic mailing list.

Anderson, T. (2001). The hidden curriculum in distance education. [Electronic version]. *Changes, 33*(6), 29.

Apple, M. (2000). Can critical pedagogies interrupt rightist policies? *Educational Theory, 50*(2), 229–254.

Aufderheide, P. (1993). *National Leadership Conference on Media Literacy.* Paper presented at the Aspen Institute, Washington, D.C.

Baran, S., & Davis, D. (1995). *Mass communication theory: Foundations, ferment and future.* Belmont, CA: Wadsworth Publishing.

Barry, A.M S. (1997). *Visual intelligence: Perception, image, and manipulation in visual communication.* Albany: State University of New York Press.

Bartolome, L.I., & Macedo, D.P. (1997). Dancing with bigotry: The poisoning of racial and ethnic identities. *Harvard Educational Review, 67*(2), 222–246.

Beyer, L.E. (2001). The value of critical perspectives in teacher education. [Electronic version]. *Journal of Teacher Education, 52*(2), 151.

Britzman, D. (1991). *Practice makes practice: A critical study of learning to teach.* Albany, NY: State University of New York Press.

Brookhart, S.M., & Freeman, D.J. (1992). Characteristics of entering teacher candidates. *Review of Educational Research, 62*(1), 37–60.

Brown, J.A. (2001). Media literacy and critical television viewing in education. In D.G. Singer & J. L. Singer (Eds.), *Handbook of children and the media* (pp. 681–698). Thousand Oaks, CA: Sage.

Brunner, D.D. (1994). *Inquiry and reflection: Framing the narrative practice in education.* Albany: SUNY Press.

Buckingham, D. (1998). Media education in the U.K.: Moving beyond protectionism. *Journal of Communication, 48*(1), 33–43.

Buckingham, D. (Ed.). (1998). *Teaching popular culture: Beyond radical pedagogy.* London: UCL Press Ltd.

Charmaz, K. (1995). The grounded theory method: An explication and interpretation. In J. Smith & R. Harroe & L. Van Lagenhove (Eds.), *Rethinking Methods in Psychology* (pp. 27–49). London: Sage.

CML. (2000). *History of the Center for Media Literacy.* Retrieved September 25, 2000, from http://www.medialit.org/CML/history.htm.

Cochran, K.F., DeRuiter, J.A., & King, R.A. (1993). Pedagogical content knowing: An integrative model for teacher preparation. *Journal of Teacher Education,* 44(4), 263–272.

Considine, D. (1997). Media literacy: A compelling component of school reform and restructuring. In R. Kubey (Ed.), *Media literacy in the information age* (Vol. 6, pp. 243–262). New Brunswick, NJ: Transaction Publishers.

Considine, D. (2000a). Media literacy as evolution and revolution: In the culture, climate, and context of American education. In A. Watts-Pailliotet & P.B. Mosenthal (Eds.), *Reconceptualizing literacy in the media age* (Vol. 7, pp. 299–325). Stamford, CT: JAI Press, Inc.

Considine, D. (2000b, September 21). Message posted to Media-l electronic mailing list.

Considine, D.M. (1997). Media literacy: A compelling component of school reform and restructuring. In R. Kubey (Ed.), *Media literacy in the information age* (Vol. 6, pp. 243–262). New Brunswick, NJ: Transaction Publishers.

Considine, D.M. (2002). Media literacy: National developments and international origins. *Journal of Popular Film and Television,* 30(1), 7–15.

Cortes, C.E. (2000). *The children are watching: How the media teach about diversity.* New York: Teachers College Press.

Cox, C. (1993). *The commission on media: Trends and issues in English instruction: Six summaries of informal annual discussions of the National Council of Teachers of English.* Urbana, IL: NCTE.

Desmond, R. (1997). TV viewing, reading and media literacy. In J. Flood & S.B. Heath & D. Lapp (Eds.), *Handbook of research on teaching literacy through the communicative and visual arts* (pp. 23–30). New York: Simon & Schuster Macmillan.

Feiman-Nemser, S. (1983). Learning to teach. In L. Shulman & G. Sykes (Eds.), *The handbook of teaching and policy.* New York: Longman.

Ferguson, R. (2000, May). *Media education and the development of critical solidarity.* Paper presented at the Summit 2000, Toronto.

Fiske, J. (1989). *Understanding popular culture.* Cambridge, MA: Unwin Hyman.

Flood, J., Brice Heath, S., & Lapp, D. (Eds.). (1997). *Handbook of research on teaching literacy through the communicative and visual arts.* New York: Simon & Schuster Macmillan.

Freire, P. (1973). *Education for critical consciousness.* New York: Continuum.

Freire, P. (1989). *Pedagogy of the oppressed.* New York: Continuum.

Gathercoal, P. (2000, May 2000). *Teacher preparation programs and media studies: Concerns about neglect, lack of expertise and knowledge of resources, and effective methods for teacher media studies.* Paper presented at the Summit 2000, Toronto.

Gerbner, G. (1995). Television violence: The power and the peril. In G. Dines & J.M. Humez (Eds.), *Gender, race, class in media: A text reader* (pp. 547–557). Thousand Oaks, CA: Sage.

Giroux, H. (1992). *Border crossings: Cultural workers and the politics of education.* New York: Routledge.

Giroux, H. (1994). *Disturbing pleasures: Learning popular culture.* New York: Routledge.

Giroux, H.A. (2000). *Impure acts: The practical politics of cultural studies.* New York: Routledge.

Glaser, B.G., & Strauss, A.L. (1967). *The discovery of grounded theory: Strategies for qualitative research.* Hawthorne, New York: Aldine de Gruyter.

Goulden, N.R. (1998). *The roles of national and state standards in implementing speaking, listening, and media literacy* (47(2)). Retrieved from UMI-ProQuest Direct 1998.

Greene, M. (1989). Social and political contexts. In M. Reynolds (Ed.), *Knowledge base for the beginning teacher.* Oxford: Pergamon Press.

Grossman, P.L. (1990). *The making of a teacher: Teacher knowledge and teacher education.* New York: Teachers College Press.

Hammer, R. (1995). Rethinking the dialectic: A critical semiotic meta-theoretical approach for the pedagogy of media literacy. In P. McLaren, Hammer, Rhonda, Sholle, David, & Reilly, Susan (Ed.), *Critical media literacy: Reading, remapping, rewriting* (Vol. 4, pp. 33–85). New York: Peter Lang.

Hamot, G.E., Shiveley, J.M., & Vanfossen, P.J. (1998). Media understandings in social studies teacher education. *International Journal of Instructional Media, 25*(3), 241–251.

Harding, S. (1987). Introduction: Is there a feminist method? In S. Harding (Ed.), *Feminism and methodology* (pp. 1–14). Bloomington, IN: Indiana University Press.

Hays, C.L. (2000, 9/14/2000). New Report Examines Commercialism in U.S. Schools. *New York Times.*

Hobbs, R. (1997a). Literacy for the information age. In J. Flood & S.B. Heath & D. Lapp (Eds.), *Handbook of research on teaching literacy through the communicative and visual arts* (pp. 7–14). New York: Simon & Schuster Macmillan.

Hobbs, R. (1997b). *The uses (and misuses) of mass media resources in secondary schools.* Retrieved December 12, 1998 from http://interact.Uoregon.edu/MediaLit/FA/MLResearch.html.

Hobbs, R. (1998). *5 questions to ask about a media message/"text."* Paper presented at the National media education conference, Colorado Springs, CO.

Hobbs, R. (1998). The seven great debates in the media literacy movement. *Journal of Communication, 48*(1), 16–32.

Hobbs, R. (2001). Media literacy skills: Interpreting tragedy. *Social Education, 65*(7), 406–411.

Hodge, B., & Tripp, D. (1986). *Children and television: A semiotic approach.* Cambridge, England: Polity Press.

Kellner, D. (1995). *Media culture: Cultural studies, identity and politics between the modern and the postmodern.* London: Routledge.

Kubey, R. (1998). Obstacles to the development of media education in the United States. *Journal of Communication, 48*(1), 58–69.

Kubey, R., & Baker, F. (1999, October 27). Has media literacy found a curricular foothold? [Electronic version]. *Education Week, 56.*

Lacy, L. (2000). Integrating standards in K-5 literacy. In A. Watts-Pailliotet & P.B. Mosenthal (Eds.), *Reconceptualizing literacy in the media age* (Vol. 7, pp. 219–275). Stamford, CT: JAI Press, Inc.

Langrehr, D. (1997). *The role of media literacy in the teacher education curriculum.* Retrieved December 15 from http://garnet.acns.fsu.edu/~dbl2291/medialit.html.

Lembo, R. (2000). *Thinking through television.* Cambridge, UK: Cambridge University Press.

Lincoln, Y.S., & Guba, E.G. (1985). *Naturalistic inquiry.* Newbury Park, CA: Sage Publications, Inc.

Lortie, D.C. (1975). *School teacher: A sociological study.* Chicago: University of Chicago Press.

Luke, C. (1998). Pedagogy and authority: Lessons from feminist and cultural studies, postmodernism and feminist pedagogy. In D. Buckingham (Ed.), *Teaching popular culture: Beyond radical pedagogy* (pp. 18–41). London: UCL Press, Ltd.

Luke, C. (2000). New literacies in teacher education. *Journal of Adolescent and Adult Literacy, 43*(5), 424–435.

Manning, P., & Cullum-Swan, B. (1994). Narrative, content, and semiotic analysis. In N. Denzin & Y. Lincoln (Eds.), *Handbook of qualitative research* (pp. 463–478). Thousand Oaks, CA: Sage Publications.

Massachusetts Curriculum Framework: English Language Arts (1997). Retrieved October 29, 2000, from http://www.doe.mass.edu/frameworks/eng97/englishS4.html.

Masterman, L. (1985). *Teaching the media.* London: Comedia.

Masterman, L. (1993). The media education revolution. *Canadian Journal of Educational Communication, 22*(1), 5–14.

Masterman, L. (1997). A rationale for media education. In R. Kubey (Ed.), *Media literacy in the information age* (Vol. 6, pp. 15–68). New Brunswick, NJ: Transaction Publishers.

McLaren, P.L. (1995). White terror and oppositional agency: Towards a critical multiculturalism. In P. McLaren, Hammer, Rhonda, Sholle, David, and Reilly, Susan (Ed.), *Rethinking media literacy: A critical pedagogy of representation* (Vol. 4, pp. p. 87–124). New York: Peter Lang.

McNergney, R. (1994). The case of Will Breckenridge. [Electronic version]. *NEA Today, 13*(3), 54.

McNergney, R.F., Ducharme, E.R., & Cucharme, M.K. (1999). Teaching democracy through cases. In R.F. McNergney & E.R. Ducharme & M.K. Cucharme (Eds.), *Educating for democracy: Case-method teaching and learning* (pp. 3–13). Mahwah, NJ: Lawrence Erlbaum Associates.

NCATE. (2002). *NCATE's Professional Standards for the Accreditation of Schools, Colleges, and Departments of Education.* Retrieved March 15, 2002, from http://www.ncate.org/2000/unit_stnds_2002.pdf

Nespor, J. (1987). The role of beliefs in the practice of teaching. *Journal of Curriculum Studies, 19*(4), 317–328.

Noddings, N. (1984). *Caring: A feminine approach to ethics and moral education.* Berkeley, CA: University of California Press.

Ohler, J. (1999). *Taming the beast.* Bloomington, IN: Technos.

Ottaviani, B. F. (1997). What about TV? A journal expands the awareness of technology's role in the classroom. *Educational Horizons, 75*(2), 90–96.

Patton, M.Q. (1990). *Qualitative evaluation and research methods* (2nd ed.). Newbury Park, CA: Sage.

Potter, W.J. (1998). *Media literacy.* Thousand Oaks, CA: Sage.

Richardson, V. (1996). The role of attitudes and beliefs in learning to teach. In J. Sikula,

T. Buttery & E. Guyton (Eds.) *Handbook of research on teacher education* (pp. 102–119). New York: Simon & Schuster Macmillan.

Rosenbaum, J.E. & Beentjes, J.W.J. (2001). Beyond the couch potato: Reconceptualizing media literacy. *Communications, 26,* 465–482.

Rummel, M.K., & Quintero, E.P. (1997). *Teachers' reading/Teachers' lives.* Albany, NY: SUNY Press.

Sanacore, J. (1997). Promoting lifetime literacy through authentic self-expression and intrinsic motivation (Reading Leadership). *Journal of Adolescent & Adult Literacy, 40*(7), 568–571.

Schwarz, G. (2001). Literacy expanded: The role of media literacy in teacher education. *Teacher Education Quarterly, 28*(2), 111–119.

Sholle, D., & Denski, S. (1995). Critical media literacy: Reading, remapping, rewriting. In P. McLaren, Hammer, Rhonda, Sholle, David, & Reilly, Susan (Eds.), *Rethinking media literacy: A critical pedagogy of representation* (Vol. 4, pp. 7–31). New York: Peter Lang.

Shulman, L. (1986). Those who understand: Knowledge growth in teaching. *Educational Researcher, 15*(2), 4–14.

Slavin, R.E., & Cooper, R. (1999). Improving intergroup relations: Lessons learned from cooperative learning programs. [Electronic version]. *Journal of Social Issues, 55*(4), 647.

Stringer, E.T. (1999). *Action research* (2nd ed.). Thousand Oaks, CA: Sage.

Sweet, A. (1997). A national policy perspective on research intersections between literacy and the visual/communicative arts. In J. Flood & S.B. Heath & D. Lapp (Eds.), *Handbook of research on teaching literacy through the communicative and visual arts* (pp. 264–285). New York: Simon & Schuster Macmillan.

Thomas, J. (1993). *Doing critical ethnography.* Newbury Park, CA: Sage Publications.

Tyner, K. (1992). The tale of the elephant: Media education in the United States. In C. Bazalgette & E. Bevort & J. Savion (Eds.), *New directions: Media education worldwide* (pp. 170–176). London, UK: British Film Institute.

Tyner, K. (1998). *Literacy in a digital world: Teaching and learning in the age of information.* Mahwah, NJ: Lawrence Erlbaum Associates.

V.S. & Associates. (1999, April). Ticker. *Brill's Content, 2,* 128.

Van den Bulck, J., & Van den Bergh, B. (2000). The influence of perceived parental guidance patterns on children's media use: Gender differences and media displacement. *Journal of Broadcasting & Electronic Media, 44*(3), 329–349.

Vygotsky, L. S. (1978). *Mind in society: The development of higher psychological processes.* Cambridge: Harvard University Press.

Weaver, J., & Daspit, T. (1999). Introduction: Critical pedagogy, popular culture and the creation of meaning. In J. Weaver & T. Daspit (Eds.), *Popular culture and critical pedagogy: Reading, constructing, connecting* (Vol. 2, pp. xiii-xxxiii). New York: Garland Publishing, Inc.

Weitz, A. (1999). *New study finds kids spend equivalent of full work week using media.* The Henry J. Kaiser Family Foundation. Retrieved March 20, 2002, from http://www.kff.org/content/1999/1535/pressreleasefinal.doc.html.

West, C. (1996). Keeping faith. In R. Reed & T. Johnson (Eds.) *Philosophical documents in education* (pp. 205–223). White Plains, NY: Longman.

Wilson, S.M., Shulman, L.S. & Richert, A.E. (1987). '150 Different ways' of knowing: Representations of knowledge in teaching. In J. Calderhead (Ed.) *Exploring teachers' thinking* (pp. 102–124). London: Cassell.

Winner, L. (1977). *Autonomous technology: Technics-out-of-control as a theme in political thought.* Cambridge, MA: MIT Press.

Worthy, J. (2000). Conducting research on topics of student interest. [Electronic version]. *The Reading Teacher, 54*(3), 298.

Yesterdayland. (2000). *New Kids on the Block.* Yesterdayland. Retrieved March 7, 2002, from http://www.yesterdayland.com/popopedia/shows/music/mu1112.php.

Index